The Girls in My Town

Carl—
My best wishes!
Yours,
Angel

River Teeth Literary Nonfiction Prize
Daniel Lehman and Joe Mackall, SERIES EDITORS

The *River Teeth* Literary Nonfiction Prize is awarded to the best work of literary nonfiction submitted to the annual contest sponsored by *River Teeth: A Journal of Nonfiction Narrative*.

The Girls in My Town

Essays

Angela Morales

© 2016 by the University of New Mexico Press
All rights reserved. Published 2016
Printed in the United States of America
21 20 19 18 17 16   1 2 3 4 5 6

Library of Congress Cataloging-in-Publication Data
Morales, Angela.
  [Essays. Selections]
  The girls in my town : essays / Angela Morales.
      pages cm. — (River Teeth Literary Nonfiction Prize)
  ISBN 978-0-8263-5662-8 (pbk. : alk. paper) —
  ISBN 978-0-8263-5663-5 (electronic)
  I. Title.
  PS3613.O665A6 2016
  814'.6—dc23
                          2015020149

Cover illustration adapted from
photograph by Steve Snodgrass, licensed under CC by 2.0
Designed by Felicia Cedillos
Composed in Palatino 10.25 / 14
Display font is Freestyle Script Std

Excerpt of "The Heaven of Animals"
from *The Whole Motion: Collected Poems, 1945–1992*
by James Dickey, copyright © 1992, published
by Wesleyan University Press. Used by permission.

For my mother, who taught me to love words

Contents

Introduction

The job of the essayist, like any storyteller, is to chase a rabbit down a rabbit hole and see where it goes. When I started writing these essays, each piece began with a single image that appeared distinctly in my mind: a bowling ball, a stack of school lunch trays, my father's gun, a dying rat, a burrito, a lost dog, a pregnant teenager, my grandmother on her deathbed. For the longest time, these images haunted me, until I had no choice but to sit down and write about them.

I discovered, then, that what began to reveal itself was a family portrait, one that allowed me to take a memory and examine it, turn it over and over. Gloria Steinem once said, "Happy or unhappy, families are all mysterious. We have only to imagine how differently we would be described—and will be, after our deaths—by each of the family members who believe they know us." Maybe, then, I wanted to understand some of the mystery of what makes a life, what makes a memory, why we remember what we remember.

As I breathed life into these essays, they became my oddly shaped children. All lined up and standing side by side, my beloved orphans are now assembled into one family portrait—one that reaches back to the childhood of my grandmother and ends with my own daughter's childhood. It's an unconventional portrait, to be sure, but hopefully it illuminates a time and place and adds another perspective to the mix.

—AM

Chief Little Feather, Where Are You?

S ome sweet evenings when the sun had left a pink tinge across the Los Angeles skyline, and Raymor Electric—my parents' appliance store—had made them lots of money, my parents would develop a manic, hungry angst that led them, in a spontaneous fit of wanderlust, to places like car dealerships and jewelry stores. This same money angst once got me a black-lacquered baby grand piano and my mother her Zsa Zsa Gabor ring, a miniature diamond staircase that cascaded across her finger. One night we drove home in a brand-new powder-blue Lincoln Continental; another night we cruised home stroking the velour seats of a rust-red Cadillac. And one evening, thanks to Raymor Electric's good fortune, my sister and I got our first bowling balls.

"Go on, pick one," my father said. My younger sister, Linda, and I studied the rows of bowling balls across the display— shiny ebony for the purist, glittery swirls for the fashion conscious.

"Come on, man, show them what you've got," my father ordered the clerk. He paced the store, checking his watch every twenty seconds while the nervous clerk fumbled with some eight- and ten-pounders.

Because of my father's short attention span, Linda and I knew that we had to choose quickly. If we didn't grab a ball and run it over to the cash register, he might suddenly decide that we were already spoiled brats with too many toys and that bowling balls were a goddamned waste of money anyway. So Linda grabbed the first one she could get her hands on—a chocolate/white swirl pattern—and I grabbed a gold iridescent ball that reminded me of space dust and the rings of Saturn.

"What about the holes?" my father said, his eyes darting across the store. "Where's the drill?"

I was always amazed at how patient salespeople could be with my father—nodding at his demands, calmly answering his rapid-fire questions. The clerk winked at us and had us stick our fingers through a series of holes in a plastic disk, and then he jotted down our measurements. In a few minutes, he'd placed each of the balls in a vise grip before lowering the chisel into the resin. When he'd finished drilling, the finger holes felt silky smooth, not bumpy and abrasive like the chipped old loaner balls we'd become accustomed to. Then the clerk engraved our names in capital letters just above the finger holes and rubbed white engraving powder in the crevices to make the letters stand out.

"Pick a bag too," my father ordered. "Hurry up! How the hell you gonna carry it without a bag?"

As fast as we could, we grabbed a couple carrying cases and ran those to the cash register too. That night, I slept with my new bowling ball, stroking it and pressing my cheek against the cool resin. I'm sure I dreamed about the weight of the ball in my hands, the fluid three-part movement of my right arm swinging back and then forward again, my right leg sliding behind the left, perfect tension across my abdomen and thighs—and hold it, hold it—the golden ball spins and curves into the headpin with magnetic force—and, yes! Another strike! A new Junior World Champion! Youngest person ever to attain a perfect score—ten strikes in a row—the elusive 300!

I first fell in love with a bowling alley when I was seven or eight years old. Back then, Raymor Electric dominated every aspect of our lives. When I was a baby, my father built a warehouse on an empty dirt lot and then turned it into a disco-style appliance superstore filled with rows of refrigerators, walls of stereo consoles with eight-track players, television sets stacked upon other television sets, endless washers and dryers.

Some people recall their childhoods back on the farm— running through cornfields or pecan orchards or pine forests, long afternoons jumping through sprinklers and camping trips with stargazing and roasted marshmallows. I remember running through mazes of washers and dryers, refrigerators and microwaves, and the glorious machine-oil-plastic-rubber smell of the inside of a new refrigerator. I remember taking long naps in an empty appliance box. Later, I would add to those memories the bowling alley that provided me with an escape from all those appliances—the bowling alley with its sugar-glazed lanes and soothing sounds of clanking wooden pins, the gentle churning of rock maple knocking around in the belly of the pinsetter machine.

Each morning before dawn, my father would arrive at the store to check inventory and send electricians out on service calls. Then he would stand in front of the store, just staring at it, like a person contemplating a sunrise or a landscape. Hundreds of light bulbs from the thirty-foot sign illuminated him as he puzzled over ways to lure more customers: Better window displays? Brighter lighting maybe? More than anything, he must have been praying that Howard's Appliance Store, his biggest competitor, would simply burst into flames—that it would explode into smithereens!

If my father was the brain of the business, my mother was the heart and the soul. Wearing cleavage-revealing jumpsuits and big dangly hoop earrings, she would stand outside the store demonstrating the latest wonder of modern technology— the microwave oven. She'd offer customers toothpick samples of her microwave-zapped hors d'oeuvres—drunken barbecued weenies and little slices of lemon pound cake. My father once said that my mother could have sold a dead raccoon. She'd say, "See? Isn't it fabulous? Just push a couple buttons, and voilà! Pot roast in minutes!"

Both my parents had grown up poor, especially my mother, whose childhood was spent traveling around California in an old, beat-up woodie. Her entire family, like Mexican Joads, slept in corrugated tin shacks at night and by day picked peaches or cotton under a blazing-hot sun. Here, then, had arrived my parents' golden opportunity to extricate themselves from poverty, to erase the past; now, if they wanted to, they could eat filet mignon every single night! We would have a Ding Dong and a Twinkie in our lunch boxes—all the same store-bought sweets our parents had been denied their whole lives. Now my father drove a Mercedes Benz or Lincoln Continental and my mother drove a Cadillac. General Electric gave us complimentary trips to Waikiki Beach, where we wore pink flowery muumuus and ate pig on a spit and macadamia-nut ice cream. What a life!

At the store my father was always making us shake hands with sales reps from big companies like Amana and Motorola— guys in polyester suits who smelled of earwax and Old Spice, guys who would chuckle when they saw us and say, "Chip off the old block, huh, Ray?"

And they were right: we'd inherited my father's stocky build, his short legs, his bowlegged gait. I'd also inherited my mother's crooked teeth and overbite, which earned me the nickname Bucky Beaver both at home and at school. "Hey, Bucky," my father would say, "would you hand me that hammer?" And my mother constantly puzzled over how to make us cuter. She gave us Shirley Temple perms and bought us red heart-charm necklaces. She bought us lip gloss and little vials of Tinkerbell perfume. She took us shopping for matching sailor outfits with gold-chain belts and wound shiny ribbons around our ponytails. No matter how hard she tried, though, sooner or later our buttons popped off our waistbands, our ribbons unraveled. We'd show up with traces of Cheetos and 3 Musketeers bars smeared across our hands and cheeks, and in front of customers or sales reps, my mother would yank us aside, rubbing at our faces with Kleenex, tugging at our pants, and whispering things like, "My God! What will people think?" or "Pull up your socks! Go wash that chocolate off your face!"

Bored out of our minds, we'd imitate my mother's microwave demos by putting on little shows for each other. We'd melt margarine with sugar and hot sauce, or whatever ingredients we could find. Sometimes, we'd throw a wad of tinfoil into a microwave and then watch it explode into lightning flashes and little sparks of fire. Other times we'd raid the secretary's desk and write stupid messages on every page of her *While You Were Out . . .* message pad. *While You Were Out . . . your boyfriend called. Message: Your butt is too big!* (ha-ha-ha!) Then we'd alter the prices on the washing machines with a black Sharpie, from $210.00 to $2,100.00 (ha-ha-ha!), and then we'd mess with the controls on all the television sets so that when my father turned on a television for a customer, all the people looked lime green.

One day Linda and I managed to empty all the quarters from the Pepsi machine by coaxing the lock open with an assortment of small tools we'd pilfered from the refrigerator repairman's toolbox. We emptied the foot-long stack of quarters into a dirty sock, and Linda was swinging it around proudly as we halfheartedly argued over how we might spend it—that Stretch Armstrong doll that we'd been wanting from the pharmacy? A bean-and-cheese burrito and apple turnover feast from Taco Lita down the street? Neapolitan ice cream sandwiches and Pop Rocks from 7-Eleven? All of the above?—when suddenly my father appeared and snatched the sock right out of Linda's hands.

"What the hell is this?" he asked, lobbing the sock up and down, weighing its value.

He scanned the warehouse until he spotted the crooked, dented Pepsi machine, money door still ajar. Electricians had been kicking it for years, and the damage had taken its toll. "Goddamn it," he said. "You robbed my Pepsi machine?"

Then he smacked our collarbones with the back of his hand, daring us to talk back. Little flecks of spit flew at us as he yelled. He started in with his usual lecture: "I worked when I was your age! I packed oranges, I built crates, I . . ." He lectured us about the roof over our heads, the shoes on our feet, and the clothes on our backs. "I give you every damn thing you need—and now you steal? From me?"

My mother, hearing the commotion, came to our rescue. She could sometimes pull key wires out of the time bomb before it exploded. She liked to make my father think that he was completely crazy, which, oddly, often calmed him down. "Oh,

Raymond," she said nonchalantly, waving a hand. "What's the big deal? It's just a few quarters."

"What's the big deal?" he asked. "The big deal is stealing. Stealing is not a big deal?"

"Oh come on, you steal from people all the time," my mother said, sighing, pushing at her cuticles.

"Goddamn you," he said, glaring at her. "I work my ass off . . ."

"We know, we know, you work your ass off. Stop overreacting. You're being ridiculous." Though my mother's you-are-so-boring routine usually made my father second-guess his anger, this time it had the opposite effect.

"You can go to hell," he said. "In fact, you can all go to hell. You little shits."

He smacked the sock down on the secretary's desk and stormed off.

After he'd gone, my mother, who'd had it with us too, turned and said, "If I were you, I'd disappear for a little while." When we didn't move fast enough, she pointed to the back door and said, "Go! Do you want him to go psycho again?"

We grabbed the sock (which turned out to have fifty-some dollars in it) and dashed out, running up San Gabriel Boulevard as fast as we could, giddy that we'd escaped. We ran past the 7-Eleven, past the Chinese liquor store, past all the cobweb-covered, abandoned insurance offices, until, like Oz, appeared San Gabriel Lanes, its geometric sign jutting over the sidewalk, framed by the purple mountains and the familiar orangey haze of Los Angeles.

Through the smoky glass doors of the bowling alley, the blond wood gleamed under dim lights, and the pins sat solid and predictable and upright.

So to escape our father and a life of appliances, Linda and I became regulars at San Gabriel Lanes, just like the old winos at the bar and those solitary, gaunt-faced men (hiding from what?) who could do the Silent Slide—the bowling maneuver in which the hand comes down so precisely, so close to the floor, that the ball makes no sound as it glides magically down the alley, rolling stealthily and forcefully with the subtlest sidespin, hooking left toward the center until the pins explode with that unmistakable, deafening *thwank!* Right into the pit! How I wished I could do that.

After the Pepsi-machine incident, my father would slip us twenty-dollar bills just to get rid of us for a while, even though he'd always say, "Do not forget. That's a loan, not a gift." Twenty dollars, back then, could buy a lot of bowling. We bowled until our arms ached and our fingers were rubbed raw. We probably could have broken the world record for most games bowled by a child in a single year. If Raymor Electric was our second home, San Gabriel Lanes became our third, and we lived in both places far more than we lived in our real home, which we saw on rare occasions, and mostly only for sleeping.

One Saturday morning I set off from Raymor Electric, lugging my bowling bag up San Gabriel Boulevard. At school my teacher had given us a flyer advertising free bowling lessons on Saturday mornings, lessons to be provided by a real, live Indian.

Sure enough, at the center of the commotion, just as the flyer had promised, stood the real, live Indian. This Indian wore a dazzling feather headdress, a white-beaded leather jacket, and real moccasins. He was tall and daunting. "Hey, kids, who likes bowling?" the Indian yelled to the crowd. Hands shot up in the air.

"Me, me, me, I do," said the crowd—a motley mix from the

neighborhood, mostly latchkey kids like us whose parents had dropped them off for an afternoon of free babysitting.

"Who wants to learn how to bowl?" More hands shot up in the air. Chief Little Feather talked about the benefits of joining a bowling league and then invited each child down to the lanes for free, personalized instruction. Gently, he held my wrist in his large hands and showed me how to angle it upward rather than sideways. He smelled like Ivory soap, and beneath his feathered tunic, I noticed that he was wearing an ordinary white T-shirt.

Between lessons, he kept pausing, saluting us, and grunting, "Howwww!" Then he'd slip back into verbose white-man talk and explain some other secret, like how to let the right leg slide behind the left leg, and how to knock off both pins when confronted with the dreaded split.

At the end of the lesson, anyone who wanted to could sign up for the Chief Little Feather League, a twelve-week commitment. I paid my two dollars and fifty cents and got paired up with a boy named Ray Yanez, a short, heavy-browed nine-year-old who didn't joke around. Like me, Ray had come to win. "Shake her hand, Ray," his mother said, pushing him toward me. "She's your teammate!" Reluctantly, we shook hands. Ray's hand was hot and sweaty, and it was the only time I'd ever actually touched a boy's hand unless you counted square dancing in Mrs. Swanson's class, which I did not.

"Hi, hon," his mother said, extending her hand. She wore lots of gold bracelets that jangled as she talked. "I'm Debbie," she said, squeezing my fingers. "Isn't this gonna be fun?" Debbie had a Farrah Fawcett hairdo, feathered at the sides and then curled into rolls of fluff that framed her face. I liked her right away.

Sometimes there were benefits to having workaholic parents.

My father certainly would have made a pass at Debbie, leering at her like a dog drooling over a pork chop. My mother might have been all friendly to Debbie's face and then later said something mean, maybe about her stupid hair or her tacky jewelry. Maybe I was just making excuses, but I was glad my parents couldn't spoil it for me.

During the next twelve weeks, all I could think about was bowling with Ray Yanez. In the darkened showroom at Raymor Electric, I studied the pro bowlers on twenty television sets—guys like Guppy Troup, who wore gold chains and sunglasses during tournaments, and women like the redheaded Betty Morris, who could play an entire game without ever once cracking a smile.

I pictured myself and Ray in those tournaments, the announcer quietly narrating our moves as Ray and I remained cool and humble, just like Guppy and Betty. Afterward, when the crowds cheered wildly, we'd remove our plastic wrist guards and bow curtly, our feathered hair blowing in the air vents' breeze.

Ray and I quickly shot up the ranks of the Chief Little Feather League. Every Saturday, I raced to the front desk to grab a copy of the dot-matrix score sheet that showed the previous week's team rankings and handicap results. While other kids goofed around and threw gutter ball after gutter ball, Ray and I kept nailing those pins. During that time, Ray and I never really spoke to one another except to mumble, "Your turn" or "Good one" or, occasionally, "Nice try." We never high-fived or jumped around because we were not, as my mother would have said, "bubbly." We were, in fact, quite the opposite of bubbly.

Though neither one of my parents ever came to watch me bowl a single game, I didn't mind. I was used to being dropped off places—movie theaters, softball games, doctors' appointments. Even without fathers and with just one mother between us, Ray and I had a ready-made audience. Those old guys with their Bloody Marys, in between drags from their cigarettes, would pump their fists and hoot and howl for us. Ray's mom, too, never missed the opportunity to yell, "Way to go!" and "That's the way to do it!" She'd beam at Ray, her pride and joy. She'd pinch his cheeks until he slapped her hand away.

I looked at our winning streak as retribution. Even if at school Ray and I were not popular or cool, at the bowling alley we ruled. Shannon Crook, a girl in my class (whose trademark was her automatically darkening glasses), had turned commenting on my ugliness into her personal hobby. She'd follow me around the playground, poking at my back with a stick and saying, "How can you live with yourself? Don't you puke when you look at yourself in the mirror?"

At the bowling alley, though, I could have torn Shannon Crook to pieces. In fact, it was usually her face that appeared as a misty apparition before the center pin. I aimed and threw hard. At times I could throw four, maybe five strikes in a row. After I threw a strike, my stomach muscles felt hard as a rock, centering and anchoring me, and honest-to-God little silver sparkles emitted from my pores.

One day after league, after Ray and his mom had gone home and the bowling alley had emptied out, I stayed to bowl a few more games on my own. With nobody to distract me, my eyes stayed closely focused on the headpin. The weight of the ball felt just right in my hands. Every ball I threw ended in a perfect strike—no wobbly pins, just pure obliteration. They went down hard and loud. With each strike, the red neon crown flashed above the pinsetter.

I couldn't believe it. Guppy and Betty and Chief Little Feather were by my side, whispering in my ear. My score began to enter the zone. I could scarcely breathe. Before that day, I'd lucked out with a high score of 202—respectable for a kid my age, but by no means extraordinary. Now I surpassed my previous score as my golden ball gleamed and spun down the lane.

In the final frames, the fever broke, but I picked up the remaining pins with dead-on spares. The final score, scrawled out in my own handwriting, totaled 274—the highest score I'd ever heard of for a kid. I stared at the numbers, reviewing my math, verifying that I'd added correctly. I wondered if I could be dreaming. And then I looked around to see if anyone had noticed. Where were the old drunk guys? Should I tell somebody? The desk clerk was busy disinfecting shoes or doing some other odd job. My heart pounded. Had anyone seen it? Would anyone believe me? Would anyone even care? If a tree falls in the woods but nobody's there to hear it, did it ever really fall at all?

At the end of the league, Ray and I won first place. It wasn't even a contest really. Chief Little Feather showed up at the awards ceremony to present us with our trophies. I was glad to see him. I thought about telling the chief about my 274 game, but I just couldn't. He seemed too remote, too adult and important and kind to risk bothering with my small news. I wasn't much of a talker anyway.

He congratulated us over the PA system and made us honorary Indians. Crowning us with feathered cardboard hats, he handed us our trophies: short pillars of fake marble with a tiny golden bowler on top. The tiny bowler was tensed up, poised to release the ball, and later he would remind me of Ray—a kindred spirit. That day, as we accepted our awards, Ray and I stood stiffly, clutching our trophies, barely smiling, eyes glued to the floor. Afterward, Ray's mother gave me a little hug, and Ray said, "Well, see you around." With my bowling bag in one hand and my trophy in the other, I lugged my ball back down San Gabriel Boulevard, back to Raymor Electric, the sun gleaming in hard pinpricks off the top of my trophy.

Without Ray and Debbie to look forward to, bowling lost some of its charm. After that, I stopped talking. Then I started crying for no apparent reason.

"Now what's the matter?" my mother said, exasperated, as if I were the kind of kid who cried every ten minutes. To my mother, dark emotions—sadness, anxiety, fear—meant a malfunction of some kind, a breakdown in the machinery.

"Nothing," I growled, choking back tears and swiping hard at my cheek with my sleeve. But instead of letting it go, she pressed on.

"Did I step on your toe? Did I poke you in the eye? What'd I do?"

"Just leave me alone," I said.

"Fine," she said.

"Good," I said, wiping away more tears.

By the time I had entered junior high, I was trying to forget about the bowling alley and the elusive 300. Even if I did bowl a perfect game, what difference would it make? Would some portal open up at the end of the alley like a door into Narnia, revealing some snow-covered wonderland dripping with icicles? Would confetti fall from the sky, and would my picture appear on the front page of the newspaper? Would my parents finally be there in the audience, cheering me on and whistling?

Suddenly, I felt embarrassed by all the hours I'd wasted. I felt embarrassed by having loved that stupid place at all. There it sat, like some nerdy boyfriend with taped-together glasses and high-water pants. I began to believe that bowlers like Guppy and Betty were not actually real people, after all, but simply actors trapped inside television bowling tournaments.

Real people with real lives only went bowling sometimes, like on Friday nights, and when they did, they brought other people along, people to joke around with.

I didn't look the same either. By eating nothing but melba toast and applesauce and swimming one hundred laps a day, I'd lost twenty pounds. I now wore lip gloss to highlight my straight, gleaming white teeth, having survived the torture of braces—tiny rubber bands and horrific metal headgear. The orthodontist declared me his biggest success. My mother's dream had come true: I finally wanted to be cute, not homely like poor Consuelo Moreno with her acrid body odor and sad orthopedic shoes. I wanted to erase my old self. In fact, I wanted to kill Bowling Girl, aka Bucky Beaver, and hide all the evidence. The last step would be to remove the last traces of her from the family photo albums.

I sneaked around with a pair of nail scissors, carefully peeling away the plastic film and removing every photo I could find with my image. I would snip around the girl in the photograph, leaving a gaping hole. I thought I was being very considerate to not cut even a sliver of anybody else. When I had finished sneaking around, most of the photo albums looked like crime scenes, like someone had stolen my body and left only the outline. Hoping that nobody would notice, I was always careful to replace the photos in their original position beneath the clear plastic film.

One day my grandmother grabbed me by the ear and dragged me to the den. My mother stood clutching a framed family-reunion photo, one in which all the relatives had posed at Legg Lake Park in El Monte—aunts, uncles, cousins, second cousins, adopted cousins, compadres. And there off to the side knelt my headless body, right next to my cousin Kristy, who smiled happily for the camera. "Sit down!" my mother ordered sharply, pointing at Grandma's sagging couch. Oh, how I dreaded what was coming.

"Who do you think you are," Grandma said, her voice trembling with rage. "How dare you destroy my pictures?" Her chin quivered; her eyes watered. Grandma did not normally cry, so I knew this was serious. She and my mother looked at me, bewildered, as though I were a stranger, some imposter.

"My God, what is the matter with you?" my mother said, horrified.

"Come on," I said, rubbing my ear, trying to diffuse the situation. "I only cut myself out."

Then they started yelling at me, calling me all sorts of names in-both Spanish and English—disrespectful and spoiled and self-centered and even the worst word they could think of: *weird*.

"This is weird behavior," my mother said. "Do you want to be a weird girl? Maybe we should take you to a psychiatrist. Maybe you need to have your head examined."

But hadn't it been my mother who had told me about the peasants in Hong Kong who demand five dollars from tourists for every picture taken? Hadn't she herself told me that some people in the world never allow their pictures to be taken because they believe that the camera is a soul snatcher? Didn't I, too, have a right to my whole self, my whole soul? I didn't understand why they didn't understand—I mean, come on, that poor girl was so ugly! I'd worked so hard to get rid of Bowling Girl, who wore husky-sized jeans and had the minor beer gut of a middle-aged man and those incredible beaver teeth, warded off with four years of braces and rubber bands, retainers and headgear.

In an Instamatic photo of the new me, I sit on a bench with my best friend, Debra. Looking like sisters, we lean in toward the middle of the frame. My shiny brown hair, worthy of a shampoo commercial, cascades past my shoulders, drops demurely over one eye as I tilt my head to the side. My fingernails are long pink ovals—no longer suitable for throwing a bowling ball! My new hairstyle requires that I flip my hair back every so often, a gesture that, at the time, I think seems very grown up. And the biggest surprise of all: my smile. Wonder of all wonders! Dr. Rhatigan, my orthodontist, had indeed accomplished nothing short of a miracle.

Then my father stopped coming home at night. I didn't miss him because he'd never really been that kind of father, the dad who came home and threw a baseball or helped us build a birdhouse, for example. My father existed more or less as a fixture inside Raymor Electric. Outside of those walls, he simply evaporated—we didn't really know him at all. My mother, though, ranted and raved, hoarding the latest evidence: a phone number scribbled on a shred of paper, a dinner receipt from a fancy restaurant, and, most importantly, a snapshot of a nondescript Asian woman wearing a beige raincoat and holding a little boy's hand. "Look at that slut," my mother would say, pushing the picture in front of us as we ate our macaroni and cheese. "She's not even pretty. What does he see in her? It must be the Oriental thing." When my father did come home, they'd step around each other in silence, glaring, and then my mother would suddenly hurl the bits of paper and shredded pictures at his face. My father would take the offensive, accusing my mother of being a prostitute, and my mother would call him a "disgrace" and a "poor excuse for a man." I hid in my bedroom and blasted Van Halen or some other heavy-metal band that could vibrate the windows and drown out every sound. Meanwhile, with nobody to steer it, Raymor Electric, like a dilapidated ship, bobbed and swayed dangerously close to the rocks.

My junior high friends and I had set a new goal for each weekend: to get as drunk as possible. Debra and Jenny, like me, wanted nothing more than to close their eyes and bob around, empty as balloons. Debra's dad appeared now and then, driving his lowrider and laying on a horn that played "La Cucaracha"; Jenny's dad seemed perpetually suspicious and tense, always hiding in the garage rigging dirt bikes to the back of a pickup truck.

We'd steal whiskey or brandy from my parents' liquor cabinet, which was stocked with full bottles of Seagram's and Johnnie Walker and Wild Turkey. My father never drank, but he prided himself on his liquor collection—usually gifts from the Maytag or Frigidaire reps. Those bottles were like his sales trophies, proof that he'd "worked his ass off." Because my father never drank, stealing his booze was easy. All we had to do was find similarly colored replacement liquids to pour into the empty bottles, and we had that part down to a science. Vodka could be water; whiskey could be apple juice, corn oil, or even corn syrup, depending on the hue. We'd pour the liquor into plastic tumblers and tiptoe back up to my room. Then we'd gulp it down, grimacing and choking until it seeped into our blood, numbing every nerve in our bodies.

One Saturday night, Debra and Jenny and I drank a whole bottle of my father's blackberry brandy. We guzzled all of it, and then Debra said, "Wouldn't it be funny to go bowling right now?" The next thing I remember is stumbling down the street and with each step thinking that the sidewalk had come up too soon as it jerked against my feet. Everything was so funny—a devil-eyed baby in a stroller, a beat-up Pinto bobbing down the road, a bumper sticker that said, "I hate fat chicks." Everything was side-splittingly hilarious, so hilarious that we could barely stand it.

At the bowling alley, I stood once again at the row of dots, balancing the ball and squeezing my eyes open and shut, trying to focus on the headpin. Bowling Girl still lived within my skin, and she was trying hard to get out. The row of alleys seesawed, and when I pulled my arm back to throw the ball, the ball fell from my fingers, landing with a dull thud. Debra and Jenny laughed hysterically, pointing at the ball, pointing at me. I laughed too, and we clutched our stomachs, cried real tears, danced around trying hard not to pee our pants. After that, Jenny's ball jumped the gutter and ricocheted off the next alley. Debra's ball pitched seven or eight feet in the air before coming down and bouncing like a basketball.

Saturday night, being league night, meant the place was filled with serious recreational bowlers, the only people left who had any respect for the sport—guys with names like Harlan and women with names like Pearl. Those old guys had most likely survived places like Iwo Jima and the beaches of Normandy and didn't much appreciate fools like us spoiling their game. They shook their heads sadly at us, or so I imagined with a defiant shame. At some point, I remember falling into a chair with my head dangling between my knees. My brain spun to the left, my stomach spun to the right. If my head had fallen off and rolled down the alley, that would have been just fine with me. It felt wonderful and awful and I didn't care if I lived or died.

Just then, a woman's sharp voice scolded, "You girls! Get out of here! It's disgusting, young girls acting like floozies! Shame on you! What would your mothers say? Get out right this second and don't come back until you've sobered up!"

I had never been kicked out of a place before. My thoughts came fast and blurry, and in direct opposition to one another: I'm sorry! I'm sorry! And, Fuck you, lady. No more fat little

Mexicans politely ordering grilled hot dogs and Cokes at the lunch counter over yonder. The world suddenly got much wider. I wished I could tell Debra and Jenny about this premonition I had that beyond the fog in which we stumbled, there lay something better: more friends, lovers, children, people who would see us, listen to us, love us, and that right there, in the bowling alley, I had glimpsed what this might mean. But when you are thirteen and drunk, you cannot see the future, no matter how hard you try, and as much as I wanted to, I could never in a million years have told Debra and Jenny about my golden bowling ball and the elusive 300, my love for Ray Yanez, or the way Chief Little Feather had so gently guided my wrist with his big fake-Indian hand.

One Small Step

By the time I'd begun the sixth grade, in 1978, "women's lib" was old news. For most of my childhood, Gloria Steinem and Betty Friedan had been pushing for the Equal Rights Amendment, and everyone seemed to have a strong opinion about the ERA—either you supported it or you were against it, no in between. Then a woman named Phyllis Schlafly—a woman whose life mission was to destroy the ERA—began appearing all over the news insisting that if the ERA passed, women would be marched into combat, homosexuals would be able to get married, and men and women would have to share public bathrooms. I figured that if Jimmy Carter and Gerald Ford supported it, as did their wives, Rosalynn and Betty (who were true ladies and not "bra burners"), what could be the harm? Even my mother, who'd grown up in a working-class Mexican family, now considered herself a liberated woman and a supporter of the ERA. To prove it, she bought books like *Our Bodies, Ourselves* and Erica Jong's *Fear of Flying*—even though in real life, my father never lifted a finger and couldn't be bothered to butter a piece of toast or wash a single dish, and each night he demanded his dinner on the table at nine o'clock on the dot.

Across my school Pee Chee folder, I had scribbled in big block letters, "ERA, YES!"—just as I'd seen on poster boards carried by women who shouted into cameras on the nightly news. We'd heard that Karen M.'s mother and father were getting divorced because Karen's mother had turned into a "women's libber" and she refused to make dinner or clean the house, and the children had to beg meals off the neighbors. According to rumor, Karen's mother, once a devout Christian, had even ditched the church. Families seemed to be falling apart—my own included—and we couldn't decide if that was good or bad.

One day my teacher, Mr. Stuebner, said, "Okay, listen up. I need six strong boys to volunteer for this year's dishwashing duties." Lara, my best friend, kicked me under the desk and mouthed, "Raise your hand." It seemed only right that if girls wanted to wash dishes at Washington Elementary School, they should be allowed to do so.

Campus jobs came with real privileges too. Girls could volunteer to answer phones in the office or tidy up the nurse's room or run around collecting roll sheets and delivering them to the office. Boys, however, could be cafeteria dishwashers—a real job that involved getting a free (and often delicious) hot lunch prepared by Dorothy, our cheerful Hungarian head cook, and working alongside a friend, and getting excused from class for at least thirty minutes, maybe longer, depending on how slowly you managed to eat after all the dishes had been washed and put away. Most importantly, working as a dishwasher resulted in a noticeable rise in social status—little kids would look up to you; teachers, kitchen ladies, and the janitors, Louie and Juan, would admire your strong work ethic and good citizenship.

But Stuebner looked at us and sighed. Normally he avoided

classroom situations that fell outside the prescribed lesson plan—that, and he must have been dreading the day that women's lib arrived at Washington School. He said, "This job is for boys. Why? It requires upper-body strength that girls don't have." Stuebner, a man who wore the same brown polyester shirt and pants every single day, held up his arm and gently flexed his biceps. Then he pointed to his arm. "See?" The class laughed loudly, partly because Mr. Stuebner's monotone voice made everything sound silly, and partly because everyone could see the flawed logic in his reasoning, given that Lara, a big Latvian girl sometimes known as Big Olga, was bigger than every boy at Washington School, except for maybe Tom Hardy, who, though large, was lethargic and flabby and could not win a race to save his life.

"But isn't that discrimination?" Lara said, over-enunciating each syllable.

Even if her behavior did not always show it, Lara was the smartest person I knew. She was really smart—I mean maniacally smart—as in builder of garage bombs or computer hacker. Lara was the only child of quiet, intense parents who had arrived in Southern California before she was born, and her father had a mysterious history involving Nazis, relatives abandoned in Latvia, and suitcases filled with counterfeit money kept under the bed. Her father, a civil engineer, spent his afternoons at the kitchen table with a pint of Stolichnaya vodka and a small, sturdy glass, not talking to anyone, just staring at the patterns in the wood. Her mother—wearing a bandanna over her hair and looking distinctly Slavic, with almond-shaped eyes and high, rounded cheekbones—watched Lara like a hawk as she managed her daughter's appointments and lessons, constantly resetting the metronome and cocking a critical ear toward the piano.

Although Lara was a genius, I had the street smarts. The

oldest of five kids, with parents who worked all the time, I was used to being home alone and taking care of myself. Unlike Lara's house, with its ticking metronome and braided rugs, my house contained heaps of headless dolls and plastic machine guns, cussing little brothers, blaring Bugs Bunny cartoons, and half-eaten bowls of Fruity Pebbles left right in the middle of the living room floor. So when Lara was periodically gripped by panic attacks, I helped calm her down. Like the time she brought her commemorative stamp collection to school and Danny G. accidentally dog-eared her 1976 Pueblo Art stamp, which had caused Lara to hyperventilate, gasping and rambling about how her father would surely kill her and how she'd be better off dead anyway, so she might as well kill herself and get it over with.

Our fourth-grade teacher, Mrs. Swanson, had bent down and whispered in my ear, "Can you take her outside?" In the hallway, I talked Lara down from her imaginary fifty-foot tree and helped her get her feet back on the ground. Mrs. Swanson had probably imagined that I had calmed Lara down by holding her hand or reassuring her that the world was still spinning securely on its axis—all very "girly" techniques. Mrs. Swanson might have been shocked to know that what I really said was, "The whole class is laughing at you! Stop being such a freak!"

"I can't I can't I can't, I'm gonna kill myself, my stamp, my stamp," Lara stuttered, breathing fast and wringing her hands. I grabbed her arm and squeezed hard.

"Bullshit! You can! Who cares about a stupid stamp? Your father doesn't care! It's just a goddamned piece of paper. Okay? Okay?"

Wounded, Lara gazed at me with fat tears dripping from beneath her steamed-up glasses. Finally, she nodded obediently, caught her breath, and wiped her blotchy cheeks with the edge of her sleeve. I refused to let her unravel, especially over a stamp. If she couldn't survive a dog-eared stamp, how would she survive the rest of her life?

"But that's discrimination," Lara said again in class.

"That's dis-crim-i-NAtion," someone said, mimicking her in a singsong voice.

"Hey, shut the hell up back there!" Mr. Stuebner said as he scanned faces for the guilty party. Years later I would learn that this was what teachers now call a "teachable moment." What an opportunity to learn about current events! What a perfect time for Stuebner to teach us about government and politics and debate! But Mr. Stuebner must have considered the topic of equal rights one can of worms that he did not want to open. He said, "Look, that's life. Life's not fair. Welcome to the real world."

Apparently, children never willingly visited the principal, because when we asked to speak with him, the office secretary, Mrs. Harris, looked confused. Mrs. Harris had been running the school office for as long as we could remember, and if women could be divided up into those with immovable hairdos and those with natural, free-flowing hair, Mrs. Harris, with her upswept beehive and thick hose that bagged around the ankles, was the former sort. She replied, "My goodness. A meeting with Mr. Crabb? Now? Well . . . let's see if he's available."

She disappeared behind Mr. Crabb's door, and after a few seconds she nodded us in. Crabbie was a salty old man with sharp features and heavy bags under his eyes, but he looked amiable enough as he gestured for us to sit down.

"Well, girls? How can I help you?" He leaned forward looking concerned, tapping a pen on his desk.

I wish I could say that we had delivered a speech of grand proportions, a speech that would have made Gloria Steinem proud. I would like to believe that we talked about progress and how if you look around, you'll see women wearing hard hats and work boots and that anything boys can do girls can do too. In reality, though, we probably said, "Um . . . well . . . um, we think that girls should be able to wash dishes. Um, it's sort of unfair that they can't." And most likely we took ten minutes to say this with all the pauses and the *ums* and the uncertain, conspiratorial glances back and forth between us.

Looking dazed, Mr. Crabb closed his eyes like he was getting a headache. He massaged his temples and said, "Hmm. I see your point. But we have to follow procedures! This sounds like a matter for student council. They'll have to vote on it! Shall we put it up on the agenda for next week?"

The student-council meeting consisted of Mr. Crabb, a few tired-looking teachers, and some bright-eyed class representatives from each grade, including a couple of second-graders who sat poised and ready to go with their sharpened pencils and notepads. Lara and I wedged our folding metal chairs into the circle and prepared to make our case. They began talking about mundane school business—money from ice-cream sales, a newspaper drive, talent-show tryouts. After each point, they paused—allowing time for the second- and third-graders to make bullet points in their notebooks. I kept wiggling in my chair and glancing at the big clock on the wall and noting every time the minute hand clicked forward. Finally Mr. Crabb cleared his throat: "Girls?"

My voice barely squeaked out, and Lara spoke, as usual, in phrases broken by long, distressing pauses. The group strained to understand us, leaning toward us, asking us to repeat ourselves and to speak up. But when one of us said the word *discrimination*, the female teachers instantly perked up.

"Bravo!" said Ms. Froelich, one of the fifth-grade teachers.

"It's about time!" She leaned forward grinning, brushing a strand of her free-flowing hair from her face. Froelich, from what our mothers told us, used to be a nun, but then she ran off with some guy and got married and then divorced him and had finally found her true calling as a fifth-grade art teacher. Her classroom—very 1969—was draped with batik prints and paintings of foreign landscapes with minarets and pyramids, and the whole room smelled like patchouli oil. In class, she insisted on being called Ms.—this at a time when the word had not yet become very common. Whenever students accidentally called her Miss or Missus, she immediately corrected them and said, "That's Mizzz Froelich. My marital status is nobody's business but my own."

Mrs. Burton, our former fifth-grade teacher, with her mild humpback and liver-spotted hands, winked and chuckled and gave us each a surprisingly hard-knuckled punch in the arm. Crabb then said, "I do have some concerns about the physical demands of the job." He mentioned the heat, the heaviness of the trays, the lifting. The teachers smirked.

"Oh come on, Leon," Froelich said. "Look at these girls."

"Let's vote," Mrs. Burton said, her eyes gleaming. Then, "Those in favor of making student jobs open to both boys and girls, say *aye*."

A brief pause, and then a murmur of *ayes*. "Nays? Objections? Discussion?"

Silence. The eager beavers jotted down some notes. "Well, then," Froelich said. "It's official."

"Way to go, girls!" Mrs. Burton said, punching us again.

Faint applause. Laughter. Meeting adjourned.

How easy was that? The vote meant that student jobs could not be assigned by gender alone, and, according to the text of the ERA, equality of rights under the law shall not be denied or abridged by the United States or by any state on account of sex. Able-bodied girls could sign up for dishwashing jobs, and boys who were by nature "people persons" could sign up to be junior secretary. Finally, boys like Brian H. could take advantage of their natural abilities—chatting on the phone and jotting down messages on those pink notepads! Boys could also now volunteer in the nurse's office—boys like Edward G. could swab the scraped knees of crying kindergartners with Q-tips and Mercurochrome! Wasn't it really about being allowed to be oneself, *Free to Be You and Me*? That's why we were not prepared for the reactions of our classmates, mainly boys who had already been chosen as dishwashers and would be sharing shifts with me and Lara in two-week dishwashing rotations.

"Dumb bitches," Tom G. said, spitting a wad of phlegm at our feet. "Fuckin' lesbos," Mike B. said, giving us the finger.

A few girls, who spent most of recess in the bathroom combing their hair and putting makeup on each other, stared at us through the mirror as they rolled on another layer of Maybelline Kissing Potion. Then one said, "We heard that you're lesbians. Is it true? Are you really homos?"

Soon, even bookish, reasonable girls like Gwen K. and Karen M. walked a wide circle around us. Nobody wanted us on their kickball teams, and you'd think we had boils or open sores or that we'd campaigned for a double homework load for every student in the school. Only the meek, soft-spoken, and bespectacled Judy Marshall surprised me by catching me gently by the sleeve and whispering, "I think it's wonderful. Don't pay attention to them."

Even unpopular boys—boys with social or physical handicaps—the same boys to whom we'd gone out of our way to be extra nice—now seemed to despise us. Even Angelo—the new kid, a strange man-boy who wore gold chains and polyester disco shirts and had a shocking amount of chest hair for a twelve-year-old—passed me a little shred of paper in class that read, "Meet me at the basketball court after school. PS: Bring your little French kiss, baby." For the remainder of class, out of the corner of my eye, I could see him leering at me, nodding his head and sliding his fingers across his gold chain.

Researchers have observed that in groups of rhesus monkeys, submissive males will occasionally stage a coup by doing something like snatching a banana from an alpha male or even attempting to kill him, and if successful, this will alter the whole social structure of the group. During this battle, loyalties of the group will shift—some monkeys will defend the banana snatcher and others will remain loyal to the previous ruler. In any case, an ugly scene ensues—shrieking and biting and eye gouging, and often at least one monkey will die. To the untrained observer, all this looks like a bunch of monkey mayhem, but to the trained eye, it will be seen as the inauguration of a new boss—a changing of the guard—the dawn of a new day.

Wearing a white apron and a hairnet, I stood at the sink behind the stainless-steel counter with one hand on the water hose, the other hand ready to catch the next lunch tray. Lara unloaded and stacked hot trays behind me, and then we'd switch places. We developed a good system this way, and it felt great to work hard and to sweat.

After eating their lunches, kids were supposed to whack their trays two or three times against the inside of the trash bin. Mashed potatoes and gravy, fruit cup with marshmallows and coconut flecks, buttered green beans, chocolate milk—all of this formed a fragrant slop inside the can. I would hose down the trays before placing each one vertically in a heavy rubber crate that I then pushed into the industrial dishwashing machine—essentially a big metal box that exploded with jets of boiling water designed to blast away every last microbe.

Each team of dishwashers worked in two-week rotations. One of the reasons the boys resented having us as dishwashers is that if we were working, they were not. One time Mike B., another dishwasher, walked straight past the trash can without bothering to whack his food into the bin. He'd poured a carton of milk into the remains of his lunch and swirled it all together into a soupy mess and then hurled it at me with all his might. He said, "Here's a little present just for you." The tray hit my chest, splattering gravy and flecks of turkey across my apron and onto my face. Eloy, Mike's best friend, also walked straight past the garbage can and then turned his tray upside down and dumped the slop onto the stainless-steel counter. The two boys then walked away snickering, their oversized twelve-year-old heads bobbing right out the door and into the playground.

Mostly, though, kids were sweet. The kindergartners and first-graders would give us their trays and then linger to watch us work. Later they'd glimpse us on the playground and wave shyly; they called us the dishwasher girls.

Teachers would wink at us when they brought their coffee mugs stained with red lipstick, which did not come off in the machine. It took forever to get that stuff off—especially Mrs. Hamilton's lipstick, which was thick as car grease. After all the trays cycled through the machine and steam-dried, we stacked them on the shelves, mopped the floor, and wiped the stainless-steel countertops. We were sweaty and exhausted. Standing in front of the roaring industrial-strength fan, we closed our eyes and let the wind blow across us. My back ached and sweat trickled down my temples, but all of it felt wonderful, worth fighting for.

In the cool, empty cafeteria, Dorothy brought us our lunch trays piled high with food—our pay for a day's work. She had served us double portions of everything—two scoops of mashed potatoes, extra turkey slices, double the gravy, two cartons of chocolate milk, and two huge chocolate-chip cookies atop a pulpy brown napkin. Over the drone of the fan, Dorothy chatted with Louie the janitor as the lunch ladies emptied the cash registers. Lunch became a leisurely affair—we'd really take our time, chatting in between bites, twirling our spoons around in the gravy.

If we had been rhesus monkeys instead of children on a playground, somebody would have needed to die. One day during afternoon recess, Lara and I were sitting under the elm tree. We liked to sit there on hot days because that elm gave good shade; that, and it was peaceful there—away from bouncing balls and the recess ladies' rabid whistles.

I can't recall the exact sequence of events, but I know it started with somebody throwing a rock at Lara's head. Hard. Then I remember that other boys had started throwing rocks too. They'd formed a semicircle around us and had apparently planned the attack, because they kept hurling rocks from their pockets, rocks that they'd obviously gathered in advance. For a few seconds we sat on the grass shielding our heads with our hands as we got pelted, and then we realized that they weren't going to stop.

I could feel the stinging imprint on my arm, my back, my leg. What had we ever done to these boys? Never hit a girl—unless she steals your job? What choice did we have but to jump up and throw rocks back at them?

Soon it became a cartoon brawl, with elbows and legs and expletives popping out of a dust cloud. Someone had me by the hair, and I elbowed that boy as hard as I could, and pretty soon Lara had pinned Mike B. to the ground and she was clutching a fistful of his greasy yellow hair, their eyes locked in a blaze of fury. Some of the social-misfit boys stood around too, saying, "Whoa, check out Big Olga" and "Go, Olga, Go!"

Suddenly, Linda the Yard Duty Lady was prying Lara off of Mike, blowing her whistle for backup. Someone had been twisting my hair and the back of my shirt collar and I unfurled his thick fingers, twisting them with all my might.

"Fuck you, you dumb bitch," Mike spat at Lara.

"No, fuck you!" Lara said back to Mike. Tears streaked a path through the dust on her cheeks. After she let him up, Mike went in for another kick and then sucked up some mucus and wound up like he was about to spit it in her face.

As I write this and place myself back in that moment, I wonder what might have been going on inside those boys' heads. These boys, after all, were good boys who came from good families. Mike B.'s mother was PTA president and sixth-grade room mother, always smiling and balancing a tray of cupcakes on her shoulder. Their parents were friendly with the teachers, and their fathers actually showed up at the Christmas pageant and the talent show. These were the same boys whose fathers helped them build elaborate models of NASA spacecraft and scale models of the California missions. What did they have to be angry about?

In the momentary lull, Linda the Yard Duty Lady turned to Lara and me with her hands on her hips, mirrored sunglasses reflecting the light: "Well, well, well. Am I shocked! Now someone please tell me. Is this ladylike behavior? Is this how ladies should act?"

Then Lara, as if possessed by some rebellious spirit, turned to Linda the Yard Duty Lady, got right in her face, and replied in a deeper-than-usual voice, "Well, Linda . . . surprise, surprise. Guess what? I ain't no lady!"

I was shocked and proud of Lara. She had used the word *ain't* and she had stood up to a grown-up. This minor miracle apparently had no effect on Linda the Yard Duty Lady, who simply rolled her eyes and then marched the four of us to Crabb's office. When he saw us, Crabb shook his head with disappointment, as if to say, I knew nothing good could come of this. It seemed too whiny, too girly, to point fingers and say, "*They* started it," or to explain to Crabb that we were simply defending ourselves, so instead we didn't say a word.

After a stern, grandfatherly lecture, Crabb informed us that he was revoking our recess for three days and if we dared to engage in any more unseemly behavior, not only would we get suspended but we would never wash another dish at Washington School ever again—and that went for all of us.

So for the next three days, when the recess bell rang, we dragged ourselves to our designated poles in the hallway. The rule was that at least one part of our bodies must be touching the pole at all times, and if we needed a drink or if we needed to pee, we had to flag down Linda the Yard Duty Lady or a passing teacher to ask for permission.

At Washington School, getting "poled" was definitely a heavy-duty punishment, mostly reserved for real troublemakers. It was hot and boring on the pole. We were supposed to ponder our crimes and think about how to be better citizens, but all I could do was watch the stream of black worker ants that detoured around my foot. The little kids looked at us curiously, with a trace of awe, or they paused to stick out their tongues and say, "Ha, ha, loser."

Crabb put Lara and Mike B. on opposing poles in front of the main office, and when I looked over at them, Mike B. was saying, "Fuck you" to Lara and Lara was giving him the finger. For three days, I watched shoes as they passed in the hallway—a whole parade of shoes. By the end of my three days, I knew who wore Nikes, who wore Hush Puppies, and who really needed new shoes. One time a mom walked by, leaned down, and said, "Hang in there, girl!" and it felt good to suffer. Maybe we were taking one for the team.

Maybe my imagination wants to fill in the gaps, but I believe a steamy unrest hovered over our playground that year, just as it hovered over the entire country. The Equal Rights Amendment had stalled out, with three more states needed for ratification. President Carter signed an extension that gave the ERA until 1982 to get the vote of the remaining three states, but time and momentum were running out. The eighties and the Reagan era loomed just around the corner.

By the end of the school year the whole dishwashing hullabaloo had blown over, and it seemed like girls had been washing dishes forever. Maybe the status quo changed a little bit— luckily without too much bloodshed. Sixth-graders had more important matters on their minds, such as junior high and the end-of-the-year dance festival.

Mrs. Swanson was the mastermind of the dance show. They called it a festival, but really it involved only one kind of dancing—square dancing—probably because it was the only kind of dancing Mrs. Swanson knew. According to Washington School tradition, sixth-grade girls were made to line up against the wall and wait passively for a boy to select them. As expected, the athletic, popular boys would choose the pretty, popular girls. The studious, smart boys would choose the studious, smart girls. And, as in real life, those of us who did not fit into one of those two categories were left to sort out our social standing. It was, dare I say, humiliating and barbaric.

Angelo the Man-Boy did his John Travolta walk right over to me and gently poked my sternum with his index finger as though he owned me.

Nobody chose Lara. She stood against the wall wringing her hands, muttering, "Oh man, this sucks so bad." Then Mrs. Swanson literally pushed lethargic Tom Hardy in front of Lara and he kept putting on the brakes, saying, "Not Big Olga. Anyone but Big Olga!"

Then during practice over the next few weeks, every time Tom Hardy do-si-doed his partner, he'd reach his hand out and then snatch it away again. Angelo the Man-Boy emitted such pungent and mature body odor that I felt dizzy every time I had to stand close to him. What's more, he was the only sixth-grade boy who already had a mustache, and he seemed proud of his manly physique.

We were depressed. Who wouldn't be? What was the point? What had we learned? Was school just meant to babysit us before we could grow up to then be mistreated by bosses and boyfriends and husbands? College was still a long way away. So at the end of the year, in silent protest, Lara and I ditched the dance festival and the sixth-grade graduation ceremony.

"To hell with them," Lara said.

"What will your mother say?" I asked.

"To hell with her too," Lara said.

As our mothers and grandmothers and possibly a few of the fathers sat on lawn chairs in the bright hot sun sipping red punch and nibbling butter cookies, Mrs. Swanson yelled greetings over the PA system. On top of everything, the teachers forced the girls to wear paper-plate hats, atop which we'd glued mounds of tissue-paper flowers. We looked like crazy ladies, like those batty old ladies from the television show *Hee Haw*. We had to line up next to our partners, like some nightmarish arranged marriage, with those paper plates tied to our heads. Just as we were about to walk onto the field to show off our square-dancing skills to all those beaming parents, Lara and I veered off behind a building and headed off down the street, leaving Tom and Angelo the Man-Boy without partners.

We dropped the *Hee Haw* bonnets into the trash can and escaped through the school's side entrance, right out of Washington Elementary School. The air buzzed with warmth and sweetness, star jasmine and roses released their heady perfume, sparrows twittered across the branches of purple jacarandas. The deep shade felt cathartic. In that brief lull between elementary and junior high we would move with slow precision, shredding rose petals and leaning against each other as we walked with no particular destination—out of a shady neighborhood with camellia bushes and green lawns and into the rest of our lives.

Gunslinging

In the days before we could dial 911, I would have to speak with the operator and ask, "Can you give me the police department?" and the same woman, each time, would reply, "Certainly. I'll transfer you now," and I would be whispering *hurry hurry hurry* and listening for the thump of footsteps behind me, and I just knew that the operator must be taking her sweet time—fumbling absent-mindedly with the cable, twirling in her chair, polishing her nails, and then finally, FINALLY, plugging the cable into the correct slot. A bored-sounding desk cop would then pick up, and I'd need to explain myself. How I despised my voice back then—so rehearsed and robotic. Those words made me ashamed of myself for failing at language, and at other things I couldn't name. I'd say, in my flat, ugly voice, "My dad is beating up my mom."

The words, though true enough, were imprecise. *My* being a descriptor of *dad* never felt altogether accurate, even though, biologically speaking, he was indeed my father, but he did not belong to me in the way that some dads belong to their daughters or vice versa. Another problem existed with the present participle verb *is beating up*, which implied that he was, at that very moment, pummeling her with his fists over and over like Rocky Balboa slugging it out with Spider Rico after Spider had already crouched in surrender and was shielding his face with his gloves. *Beating up*, although accurate to a degree, did not capture the subtlety of the day after day—the constant mind-numbing nature of the fight, the petty haranguing, the ebb and flow of the action itself: first escalation, followed by climax and, to use literary terms, a denouement—followed always by eerie silences and another surprise climax, no resolution in sight. Furthermore, the object of the sentence—*mom*—was the passive vessel upon which the subject (*dad*) was acting. In addition, the verb *beating up* implied that Mom was further being acted upon and unable to fight back, which to an extent was certainly true but did not adequately portray my mother as a three-dimensional human being with free will and an ability to make choices, both good and bad. (Consider: the Ex-Lax hot chocolate; a box of sugar in the gas tank.) Of course I could not have articulated any of this at the time, though I am certain that this is how I felt.

Anyway, after I said that initial sentence, "My dad is beating up my mom," the cop would say, "Stay on the line with me, okay?" and I'd say, "Um. I really can't." The cop, then, so as not to reveal alarm, would say, "Listen, if you need to hang up, go right ahead and do that. We're on our way." Minutes later, as promised, two barrel-chested police officers would appear on our front porch, rapping on the front door with their billy clubs, their gorgeous badges gleaming in the sunlight. *Police Officers! Open Up!*

One time my mother looked at me and sighed, disappointed

that I'd called the police. She told me that, actually, I should have called my father's parents instead of the police. Her logic: at least his parents would feign disgust. They'd judge him and use words like *shame* and *disgrace*. *Es la verguenza!* The police, she reasoned, would only further infuriate my father. He'd get thrown into a jail cell; he'd call his brother Eddie; Eddie would bail him out; he'd return home, madder than ever.

Also, my mother hated having to give a report to the police and then having to decide whether or not to press charges. She'd always be wearing nothing but a thin, clingy nightgown, no time to grab a robe much less put on some lipstick or drag a brush through the hair. Plus, they'd want to examine her bare arms, her neck. Plus, our neighbors on Country Club Drive seemed to enjoy standing on the sidewalk and staring at the police car and our house—children and adults alike. In our all-white neighborhood, they would gather with crossed arms, squinting beyond the sun's glare toward our front door, acting like they were 100 percent entitled to stare, as if staring at my house and whatever emerged from it were no different than staring at elephants in the zoo. My mother said that they thought we were a bunch of dumb, dirty, low-class Mexicans. But I did not care. I liked the handcuffs, the starched black uniforms, the static of the radios clipped on to the shoulders, and the contrast between the supposed good guys and my father—in his threadbare Hanes T-shirt, polyester pants, and work shoes, no socks—who always emerged from our house looking like an escapee from the local mental hospital as he was led to the back of the patrol car.

These police officers—always male—went out of their way to be nice to me. They talked in soft voices and asked for my side of the story. They sat with me on the couch, pens in hand, recording all my words onto little notepads. They said things like, "Don't be afraid to tell the truth." I felt vindicated then, even if only for a few minutes, knowing someone had listened to me and that someone could hear about the things I'd been seeing for years on the other side of our fat yellow roses and lush lawn.

But my mother was right. What good were those accounts, in the end? My words seemed to have evaporated into thin air. I didn't know what it meant to press charges or why the police did not lock up my father for more than a few hours at a time. Soon I learned that calling the police was useless, even more dangerous. And if my father always came right back home, faster than zombies in *Dawn of the Dead*, what was the point?

One day I called up the other set of grandparents—my mother's parents—and minutes later, Grandpa screeched up in his rattling, beat-up Ford pickup truck. When my father opened the front door, Grandpa pointed his hunting rifle directly at my father's face. Grandpa's hands were shaking, and he said, "Son of a bitch." I stood there, frozen in place and dumb as a potted plant, half-hoping Grandpa would pull the trigger, fascinated by my father's rapt attention.

Not long after that, I pulled out the drawers of my father's built-in dresser, climbed them like a ladder, and reached around in the highest cabinet until I felt cool gunmetal—his .22 pistol. I pulled it out and, balancing on the edge of a drawer, pointed the gun at my father's back as he held my mother by the hair. "Hey," I said, wanting to give him fair warning. (Never shoot a man in the back—I knew that much.) When he turned around, he did a double take. His face went suddenly slack and pale, but he chuckled nervously, and I too had earned his rapt attention, maybe for the first (and last) time in my life. Just like in all those Clint Eastwood and Charles Bronson movies that he had taken me to see (although I would have much preferred *The*

Apple Dumpling Gang or *The Shaggy D.A.*), I said, "One move and I'll blow your goddamned head off." He said, "Ha-ha, Angie, that's funny. Now put that thing down. That's not a toy. That thing's for real."

"No shit," I said, steady on the aim, just like I'd learned from Charles Bronson, right between the eyes. I felt that I'd been pushed to the edge of a cliff—I felt crazy from the aforementioned ebb and flow, like I wanted to live on dry land, no ebb, no flow. I did not really want to kill him. I just needed him, at that moment, to be erased from my life. From our lives. "Okay, not funny," he said. "Quit fooling around now. I'm serious."

My finger grazed the trigger—a lovely, terrifying pulse, no tension, just a fraction of an inch of free fall and then slight pressure—the threshold between one existence and another. Will it be curtain number one or curtain number two? Of course I did not know a thing about guns, whether they needed to be cocked or whether they came with some safety latch, but the expression on my father's face suggested that I was, indeed, on the right track. As I balanced on the edge of the drawer between two possibilities—my eyes on my father, my finger poised on the trigger—my mother appeared white and glowing in my peripheral vision. She glided closer, soft as a ghost, and said somewhere near my left ear in a low, gentle voice that made me look at her—for the certainty and conviction that I had heard in her words had startled me from my gunslinging trance—"Listen to me. Do NOT ruin your life. He's not worth it. They'll take you away to Sybil Brand and I'll never see you again."

I knew Sybil Brand, all right. Sybil Brand, a maximum-security prison for women, housed criminals like Susan Atkins, member of the Manson family. We'd always driven by that massive hilltop structure en route to my paternal grandparents' house. Sometimes we'd see sixty-mile-per-hour flashes of orange-jumpsuit–clad women outside in the yard, many of them leaning against a barbed-wire fence, probably bragging about their crimes. I'd always feared that one day my mother would end up there, the syntactical structure being, *She shot him*, rather than *He shot her*—"she" being the actor, "he" being the acted upon. I was surprised, then, by my mother's warning, for I had not thought that I could end up in prison too. Children must assume that because they are children, adults will protect them no matter what, even if they have killed someone. And perhaps I hadn't thought that this sort of killing was actually a crime; I had just thought of shooting my father as a practical solution to an ongoing problem. So in deciding whether or not to pull the trigger, I suddenly glimpsed myself— clear as a photograph—youngest girl in Sybil Brand—*Eleven- Year-Old Girl Shoots Father*. How quickly the brain weighs the pros and cons. Pros: he's gone. Cons: an explosion, blood splatter, sirens, police, child psychologists, a trial, traumatized siblings, a distraught mother. I'm led from the house in handcuffs, head bowed, neighbors watching. Like in those dreams when one person is at the same time another person, I would become my father, he would become me.

I remember how he stood there reaching for the gun and breathing heavily, his bloodshot eyes darting back and forth, his life one of take, take, take, a person as mysterious to me as any stranger. I knew then that I did not want his life—it would have to end some other way. My dogs needed me. My brothers and sisters needed me. He had owned much of my childhood, but I would not give him my future.

The Big Divorce

That year—1978—Vietnam had invaded Cambodia, *Annie Hall* would win Best Picture, and "Macho Man" by the Village People was in the top ten. At night I would study colorful maps of Asia as they appeared on the nightly news—maps in which each country appeared bright and elementary, no shading or topography whatsoever. I worried about the shifting boundaries and how one country could so easily invade another and how easily these invasions could spread until soon, it seemed, everyone would be invaded and conquered. Also, at this time, Gloria Steinem was making calm, mind-boggling statements like "Some of us are becoming the man we wanted to marry!" and before that, Bella Abzug had famously declared with an upraised fist, "A woman's place is in the house—the House of Representatives!" Thirty-five states had ratified the Equal Rights Amendment and three more states were needed to amend the Constitution.

All this talk about invasions, defending borders, and fighting for rights must have inspired my mother to finally take her five children and run away from an abusive husband. For months—years maybe—Helen Reddy had been singing the soundtrack to my mother's life.

En route to Lucky Supermarket or Washington School or to the dry cleaner to pick up my father's laundry, my mother would pop in her Helen Reddy eight-track cassette tapes and turn up the volume full blast. Then, all of us, even my younger brothers, would sing along at the tops of our lungs, "I am woman, hear me roar!" With the windows rolled down, we sang with gusto, without a trace of embarrassment.

Once, without telling my father, my mother had taken me to a celebrity auction in Hollywood, proceeds to be donated to a battered-women's shelter. That day an item up for auction was one of Billie Jean King's tennis dresses, supposedly one she wore at Wimbledon. When the bidding was in full swing, my mother's arm shot up and she shouted her bid. I was surprised, because my mother couldn't care less about tennis or sports in general. Then, every time the auctioneer raised the price, my mother raised her hand and kept right on bidding. Finally I heard, "Sold to the lady with red hair!" I don't remember how much she paid for the dress, but I know it was *hundreds* of dollars.

"You are so weird!" I said afterward. "Why on earth did you do that?" She shrugged. "I just felt like it. I don't know what came over me!"

Like coconspirators, we carried the dress home in its filmy plastic and tucked it deep inside my mother's closet where my father would never find it. If he had found it, here's what he would have said: "Have you lost your fucking mind? You wasted money on this piece of crap? So you're a lesbian now?"

In those days, Billie Jean King, tennis-player extraordinaire, was living proof that women did not have to put up with that kind of shit. I can still see that dress—ironically feminine—heavy, multilayered cotton eyelet and lace trim, pink monogrammed sweater embroidered with the letters *BJK*, pearl buttons and lace embroidery around the collar and around the elastic of the built-in underwear.

But that dress exuded *power*. And like a talisman, it seemed to radiate some sort of protective aura. Therefore, I liked showing it off to babysitters and cousins, or to anybody who would look at it, though I never dared to try it on.

We knew that one day Ms. BJK would be dead and we'd have her tennis dress—valuable, not for money, of course, but as real historic memorabilia. Imagine having the actual dress of Elizabeth Cady Stanton or Lucretia Mott! Here was history in the making!

Every so often I'd slide open my mother's mirrored closet doors to borrow a sweater—and when I saw that tennis dress wrapped in its delicate plastic sheath, I'd have to pause for a few seconds just to admire it.

———

That summer, mornings began with a windless blue sky and spotted mourning doves fluttering down the eaves. Those gentle birds soothed us back to sleep with their melodic cooing, as did the neighbors' oscillating sprinklers, which made a pleasant *shush-shush-shush*. By the time I'd awakened, my parents would have already gone to the shop—Raymor Electric and Appliances. My father, a chronic insomniac, would have arrived long before dawn to unlock doors, turn on lights, and await the arrival of his electricians. My mother would have taken my younger siblings to the babysitter and then she would have joined my father to answer phones and to charm the customers into buying a washing machine or refrigerator or microwave oven. So in our parentless house on Country Club Drive, my nine-year-old sister, Linda, and I could do as we pleased.

Sometimes my parents wouldn't return home until nine o'clock at night, and by that time my father would have already picked a fight with my mother and they'd be locked in the middle of it when they walked through the door. Typically, he'd accuse her of having committed various crimes that day, such as flirting with the Motorola sales rep (or the newspaper ad guy, or the gas station guy, or any guy for that matter). My father would claim to have seen how she'd looked at that Motorola guy with her cow eyes and how that guy's eyes had been popping out all over her cleavage, and did she enjoy that, acting like a slut? Dressing like a slut? Did that feel good? Did that turn her on? Is that how a good wife should act? And, by the way, why had she stolen money from his wallet? So she could go buy more slutty clothes so guys like Mr. Motorola would keep drooling over her?

My father kept us all on edge—a common expression being walking on eggshells, though walking on nails would have been more accurate. The police had visited our house more than once, and after they'd taken my father to jail to cool off, I would say to my mother, "Just get a divorce! Why do you put up with this? What are you waiting for?" I yearned for a divorce, for it would be my divorce too; I even liked the word *divorce* for its clean beauty—the effortless cut of a sharp knife—a naked ankle freed from a steel trap, a hemp rope loosened from the neck.

———

So most days that summer when I was eleven years old, Linda

and I spent the better part of the day home alone and playing dead in our swimming pool. In that shimmering, turquoise expanse, we'd let our bodies go limp, our hair swirling around our faces like jellyfish tentacles. Suspended and weightless, we'd pretend to be lost at sea. One of us would churn up the water into magnificent waves and foaming eddies while the other bobbed around trying to hold steady in a fetal position. Inevitably, in those years of shark and disaster movies, we'd imagine great white sharks: massive, chomping bloody gums and rows of razor teeth. Of course we knew we were idiotic to imagine that great white sharks could attack us in our very own swimming pool, but when you are eleven or nine and home alone, pools easily become oceans, and the mere idea of a shark is enough to send you running to dry land. So with sharks swimming round in our heads and with our lungs aching from too much LA smog, we'd hoist ourselves out of the water and flop down onto our bellies, foreheads resting on balled fists. The hot solid concrete burned our legs and made us shiver. Even now, remembering those days, I hear my erratic breath echoing against the ground; I feel my heart beating steadily inside my eleven-year-old chest, and I see those glistening droplets of water shrinking and evaporating off my forearms.

That summer felt like a slow-moving creek—like water that had meandered into a dead-end tributary—stagnant, but rich with flutters of algae, water striders, and rock beetles. So in our own little tributary, we dozed in the sun and sprawled out across our sticky, faux-leather couch, on which we watched game shows galore—game shows until our eyeballs ached— *The Gong Show* or *$25,000 Pyramid* or—our favorite—*The Price Is Right*.

Large-breasted housewives bounced up and down on stage,

twirling their jumbo cardboard checks and ogling their new Buicks. We liked to see who would win the Showcase Prize or the "European Fantasy," usually consisting of a whole slew of related prizes—plane tickets to Paris, a set of Samsonite luggage, a 35mm camera, an oil painting of a Swiss chalet, dinner on the Eiffel Tower. A prize like that could be worth $20,000!

The redheaded model, Holly, sashayed her hips and rubbed up against the suitcases, gently massaging the items with her fingertips, as the male announcer, Rod Roddy, described each item. The first female contestant leaned into the microphone and bid boldly: $2,000.

"Higher!" we yelled. "Come on, higher! Higher!"

Rod Roddy would reveal the actual price of the items: $5,500! Then the winner's podium lit up, miniature light bulbs flashing madly, bells dinging. The winner hooted and howled and sprinted up to the stage, where she danced a little jig and lunged at Bob Barker, practically knocking him down as she kissed him violently on the cheek.

We'd peer into the television screen as these people dissolved into a million disconnected dots.

Television exposed us to hours of hysterical women bemoaning their clogged sinks, distraught women puzzling over whether to serve stuffing or potatoes, robotically happy families biting into Big Macs, and sexy women seducing men with their irresistibly silky L'eggs panty hose. So when our heads spun with a cacophony of advertising jingles ("Roto-Rooter, that's the name, away go troubles down the drain!") and we felt inexplicably depressed from staring at too many laughing, fun-loving families, we'd abandon the TV and cherry-bomb ourselves back into the pool. Or maybe I'd disappear into my bedroom to read a Stephen King novel or to write a letter to Ufuk Ufuk, my Turkish pen pal from Istanbul (whose name, I enjoyed telling people, was definitely pronounced You-fuck You-fuck). I'd bolt my door before Linda could slip in behind me, and then she'd body slam it or kick it until I relented and let her in.

———

Just when it seemed summer would never end, our slow-moving creek began to rise. One morning after my father's car had disappeared down the driveway, my mother woke us up by shoving Hefty garbage bags into our arms and saying, "Get your clothes! Quick! We don't have much time!"

"Why? What are you talking about?" I said, confused by my summer-induced stupor.

"We're moving," she announced. "We're getting the hell out of here."

"Right now? Today?"

"I've got it all planned out," she said. "Hurry up now—get dressed—march!"

My mother moved with quick, militaristic precision, as if she'd been rehearsing our escape for months. We stumbled around the house picking up dirty clothes or any object that lay in our paths—a single shoe, a headless doll, a rusty screwdriver. Then my mother's sister Delmira arrived to assist in the getaway. We kept glancing around, praying that my father wouldn't come home, knowing that if he did, he'd go 100 percent berserk. He was that kind of man. Consequently, the packing up happened so quickly that in a few minutes my mother and Auntie Miri had gutted the kitchen and the bathrooms with whirlwind force—they'd left cabinet doors flung wide open, with clumps of tattered receipts and plastic cups strewn across the linoleum.

At one point, Auntie Miri kicked off her shoes, and for some reason I still recall how her long, crooked toes gripped the concrete and how her foot bones fanned out as she ran awkwardly across our backyard, balancing in her arms a stack of our indestructible, Butterfly Gold Corning Ware. Funny, the details you remember in moments of high drama, as if, in rebellion, the brain slows down and refuses to process more than a single snapshot at a time.

"Come on, shake a leg! Hustle!" they kept saying, nudging us forward like we were baby horses and the barn was on fire.

Finally, we'd crammed the Suburban so full that the doors barely latched shut. All five of us squeezed in together on top of the mounds of Hefty bags, with my baby sister, Monica, wedged next to the vacuum cleaner, my brother with his elbow inside the blender. My mother then slid into the driver's seat, took a final glance around, skidded out the driveway, and away we went. Suddenly my six-year-old brother threw his arms up and wailed, "But WHY??"

I could see my mother's stony reflection in the rearview mirror. Ignoring my brother, she stared straight ahead. So sudden was our departure, we scarcely had time to think about what we were leaving behind and what it all meant.

———

We drove onto the freeway and headed north out of Los Angeles, as my mother mumbled phrases like "A new life," "A fresh start," "A second chance." Stark silhouettes of cholla cactus and yucca trees began to rise up across the high-desert landscape. Tumbleweeds rolled across the highway as a low summer sun streaked the evening sky with heartbreaking slashes of pink and orange. The horizon opened up then, wide and endless, and I felt a twinge of terror at the prospect of so much open space. We knew that this—whatever this was—was going to be big. The prospect of never seeing my father again gave me both great relief and great uncertainty. I began to wonder if he was really the ogre I'd made him out to be—or if maybe somewhere in there was a nice man, a man who could maybe act more like the fathers on television. Maybe we were making a gigantic mistake, disappearing so suddenly—as if aliens had sucked us up without a trace.

In a dusty desert town, my mother drove us into a quiet neighborhood of sixties-style flat-roofed houses, where some kids were kicking a ball around, a guy was washing his car. She slowed and stopped and then bumped up into the driveway of one such house, first and last month's rent already paid.

For months she'd been stashing away grocery money and concealing her escape plans, lest one of us should blab to my father and spoil everything. The plan: we'd hide out here, she would file for divorce, and when alimony was settled and property had been divided, we would move back to LA. She did not want my father to go psychotic. She knew that once he got those divorce papers, he'd hire a private investigator (or a hit man), whatever it took. She didn't want to hide at a battered-women's shelter. More important: she didn't want us to grow up without a mother!

During my father's darkest moods, he'd pace the house, guard the doors, hide the car keys, stalk my mother around the house. The two guns were a problem—one that he kept wedged under the seat of his car and that other one stashed on the top shelf of his closet. I could definitely imagine him shooting my mother, or possibly all of us, like those men in the news who'd lost their minds from the pressures of modern life—failing businesses, mortgages, medical bills, whining kids, barking dogs. They'd simply gone off the deep end. My father could have been one of those.

So when my mother would start whispering about battered-women's shelters—these places where women could supposedly hide from their abusive husbands, so they couldn't be tempted by husbands who would sweet-talk them and bring them presents and then drag them home by the hair—I'd worry. Certainly, I did not want my father to hurt my mother. But I also knew for certain that I did not want to live in a battered-women's shelter. For one, I hated the terminology.

"Battered" seemed ridiculous. Wasn't "battered" how one described an old shoe or smashed-up car? And wasn't it true that unlike women, shoes and smashed-up cars did not have brains or free will? And wasn't a "shelter" actually a place for stray dogs and cats—a chain-link prison camp for animals where the thin, sour odor of fear permeated the air—a scent that made you feel terribly sad? How did any of this apply to people? How did any of this apply to us? If my mother wanted to leave, I thought, then she should leave! If she wanted to divorce my father, then she should just do it and quit thinking about it! Obviously, I understood very little about the human heart and basic economics.

In our getaway house, the last shards of desert twilight fell across the empty rooms as we crept around our new house. We stuck our heads into closets and pried open jammed windows. The whole place, including knobs and hardware, had recently been coated with a thick, sloppy layer of white latex paint. Traces of other people's smells seeped through—cigarettes, perfumes, cats. One might say that the house itself was battered. An empty house, though, is an utterly beautiful space—akin to a blank page across which any words might soon be written.

Without my father's enormous, suffocating presence, we felt untethered and silly, like we should dance and sing. We turned on the transistor radio as we unloaded the Suburban, humming to disco tunes and bobbing around the tiny house. Later we spread sheets across the gummy carpet to make temporary beds. My brothers and my mother slept in one room, and my sisters and I slept in the other. It felt like one crazy adventure, yet I could in no way fathom the idea of permanence. I didn't sleep, however, being worried about bugs in the carpet, where I'd go to school, whether or not my father would bother to open a can of dog food for Caesar and Cleo, and, most of all, whether my father would, any second, come banging down the door, hell-bent on having us back, ready to drag us home.

The next morning we got dressed and looked at my mother: Now what?

"I'll go get some groceries," she said cheerfully. She came back with the usual processed foods to make us feel right at home—Oscar Mayer wieners, SpaghettiOs, macaroni and cheese, Frosted Flakes, Twinkies, a gallon of milk. She also brought coloring books and crisp boxes of brand-new crayons. Then she left me in charge while she went out to look for a job. She'd once owned her own beauty shop—La Candesa—and she knew the beauty business inside out.

"We can do this," she said. "It won't be easy, but we can do this." And I believed her. After she left, I sat at the kitchen table with Linda, Rocky, Chris, and Monica, all of them eerily subdued and trying so hard to be good. Their chubby fingers grasped at the pristine crayons as they filled in cartoon shapes, and I knew I would have to grow up fast.

The last tenants had left some kitchen curtains—threadbare, happy ruffles in a yellow-and-white checkered pattern. They flapped gently in the hot breeze. My mother would not have bought curtains like that, but they seemed a good symbol of our new life. I practiced saying to myself, *My mom and dad are divorced. My parents got a divorce.* Terrifying thoughts crept up then—visions of my mother actually going out on dates with guys like the Motorola rep, guys wearing soggy leisure suits who smelled of scotch, Old Spice, and cigarettes. I imagined my mother drinking champagne and laughing at all the jokes, pretending that the Motorola guy was hilarious. Even though I had no evidence to prove that my mother would become a party animal, I imagined strange men invading our desert hideaway—playing mean jokes on us, calling us "kid." Oh my God, I thought. What if she remarries and we get a stepfather? Stepfathers did not have the biological connection that real fathers had—and even if real fathers could be complete assholes, they had their DNA to protect, whereas stepfathers had nothing to lose. In fact, a stepfather would want to make new babies, and where would that leave us? That possibility had never before crossed my mind when I'd dreamed of divorce.

———

At El Dorado Elementary School, sounds and smells of sweaty children and ammonia-scented hallways, though normally depressing, soothed me with a bland familiarity—pink rubber erasers, pencil shavings, that beef stroganoff smell wafting from the cafeteria. Subconsciously, I must have believed that if my mother could reinvent herself, I could reinvent myself too. Nobody would know that I'd once had a terrible overbite or that I'd once been a fat girl; that is, before all the swimming and the Figurine diet bars. Now I could be the smart girl, or the mysterious girl—or any kind of girl really.

Back at the getaway house, I stacked my new textbooks on our kitchen table. I vowed to improve my terrible penmanship and to study harder in math. I would keep my pencils sharpened to dangerous, precise points. While my mother boiled weenies and sliced them into Franco-American spaghetti, I cut out little flash cards and memorized my vocabulary words, words that very well might have been *displacement, alienation, fortitude, optimism.*

We set up our small television set atop the creepy shag rug in our new living room so that my brothers could watch *Hawaii Five-O* or *The Six Million Dollar Man.* Monday nights, though, were mine: I would have conniption fits if I couldn't watch *Little House on the Prairie* and *The Waltons.* I was obsessed with these old-fashioned family dramas—stories with simple morals, braided rugs, and homemade pies. As much as I loved television, I longed for a house without one—a time when Christmases meant a heart-shaped sugar cake, an orange, and a shiny new penny. Best of all, my television shows provided me with surrogate fathers: Charles Ingalls became my top choice, for he could build log houses, play the fiddle, give bear hugs (even to other men), as well as spin a good yarn. And someday, my boyfriend would have to be just like John-Boy Walton—aspiring writer and lover of poetry (and small furry critters), kind to all people, regardless of color or creed. I never doubted that somewhere a real John-Boy existed, even if I had never met one. Maybe though, what I really wanted was not to be married to a John-Boy but to *be* a John-Boy—to always do the right thing, to take good care of my brothers and sisters, and to find a voice with which to tell my future stories.

———

Then one day, just as we were making friends at school and settling into a routine, my mother said, "Hey! Let's go get some ice cream." In the blazing heat, we climbed back into the Suburban and drove to 31 Flavors, where I got my usual scoop of pink bubblegum ice cream. My brothers and sisters ordered their rainbow sherbets and fudge ribbon swirls and strawberry shortcakes. Then we got back into the car and were so busy licking away at our ice cream that we did not notice that my mother had driven straight onto the freeway and that our car was moving at top speed—not headed back to our little flat-roofed house but somewhere else entirely. Some force had overtaken her—some sudden breakdown of willpower (similar to how an alcoholic decides to drive to the liquor store)—and she went into that trance, once again.

"Uh? Hello? Where are we going?" we said, looking all around. My mother didn't say a word but kept right on driving. She was concentrating hard on the road ahead, her fingers gripping the wheel. With ice cream running down our arms, we watched the yucca trees begin to shrink in the rearview mirror, and we didn't dare say a word. After a while we saw the *Now Entering Los Angeles County* sign as we descended out of the mountains and straight into a third-stage smog alert, into the rumble and whistle of traffic, and finally we were right back in it—inside that pillow of brackish, brown haze that engulfed Los Angeles and would soon engulf us for the rest of our childhoods.

Then there it was: Raymor Electric and Appliances—Reddy Kilowatt light-bulb man flickering on and off, on and off, and suddenly there he was—my father—vivid and three-dimensional, throwing open the car door and crying like a baby into my mother's lap, crying about how much he'd missed us, saying how much he'd rather be dead than to live without us. *Sorry, Sorry, Sorry!* Too overwhelming were the emotions of that moment, so thick with hope and regret and anxiety, the Suburban might have plunged into a lake and we might have been swallowing water, all of us quietly resigned in our fate to live forevermore without oxygen.

I had to turn away.

But I saw that my father was human, after all. I remembered a time when he'd once showed me the stars, when he did not rage, when I saw glimpses of that other man he had decided not to become. I learned, then, that being human is no easy task. Families were simply random people—forget genetics, forget blood—just random people, all of us thrown together to eke out an existence, all our flaws, all our trepidations.

But what would become of our little house in the desert? What about El Dorado Elementary School, my embryonic yet blossoming friendships, and my new textbooks with their unbroken spines? What about Helen Reddy's "You and Me Against the World"? I'd felt real despair then, and I knew that his win had been our loss. He'd regained a family and we'd failed at a divorce.

Oh, how I longed to be a dog! My life would be so simple: gnaw a good bone, bite at a couple fleas, doze in brilliant, blinding sunlight, then take a good roll in the grass. Instead, life was turning out to be a kaleidoscope of emotions—emotions for which I had no name. But I was glad to be going home; I had to admit, living on the fringe felt derelict and lonely. I missed my dogs, the mourning doves, the sprinklers, the swimming pool—all those things that lulled us into believing that we could go on like that forever.

Skin and Toes, Ears and Hair

I

When I was eight years old, I woke up on Christmas morning to find that Santa had left me a new bicycle—a pristine, white Schwinn—complete with a silver-glitter banana seat, built-in handlebar tassels, a horn, and a basket decorated with bubblegum-pink flowers. That bicycle, I would soon learn, would provide me with my ticket to freedom—my first real view of the big blue horizon—no little brothers, no little sisters, no barking dogs—just wind in the face and plenty of asphalt. Roads, then, seemed to symbolize the future. Everything that a person could accomplish lay somewhere on those roads—best friends, good deeds, prizes, dogs, and farther down the road, husbands, children, houses, more dogs. I wondered how far I might go and still find my way back. I rolled down our drive-way, rounded the corner, and began my life.

Up and down the blocks I'd ride, cutting through large sections of a map that appeared in my head, first around the big blocks and then slicing them up, road by road. Beyond our street rolled out a grid of more houses, then apartment buildings interspersed with strip malls, all blurring together mile after mile—suburbs of Los Angeles without clear-cut boundaries, no common center. I would pedal, pedal, pedal, past liquor stores, past supermarkets, past parked cars, past trees all ablur, unaware of exactly where I was going.

One Saturday I decide to maneuver into a narrow gap in a chain-link fence—a pedestrians' entrance to an elementary school that is not actually my school, but familiar nonetheless for its lima bean–green walls and hallways scented ever so faintly with vomit and pee. On the empty school grounds, I can ride undisturbed through the long, cool hallways without some recess lady or teacher to chase me away. The cement beneath my tires feels smooth as ice. Those hallways become my own racetrack, where I can test my speed and agility as I skid around sharp corners, kicking back hard on my brakes. Arcing out onto the oily blacktop playground, I do some figure eights and then glide back into the hallways, pedaling, pedaling, my leg muscles burning gloriously.

I could play alone for hours, only semiconscious of the world around me. Assuming that adults and children occupied separate orbits, I believed that I was mostly invisible. In my mind, grown-ups needed to tend to their business, just as I needed to tend to mine. I liked to think that if all the adults should die suddenly in some adult-only plague, I could have survived very comfortably, much more naturally than other girls and boys my age, whose parents hovered nervously over their heads, fussing over them, fretting over their every move. I used sharp knives and can openers, gas flames, and medicines. I could change a diaper, make a bottle, ride a bus, and push my brothers and sisters in their strollers for miles. I shopped at the grocery store, fed the animals, ate anything I pleased, and finished my homework without a parent nagging me about it. I knew that my life belonged to me and that if wanted a good life, I would have to work hard. This unbridled freedom of mine came as a result of my parents' long work hours at their ever-growing appliance store. To me, that store was like an enormous ship, its wheel spinning madly, sails flapping in the wind, and they were the hands on deck, each day, struggling to control it. I knew that they would never get off, not until the deck was cracking apart and the ship was underwater. Meanwhile, then, with my parents preoccupied, I could pretty much roam anywhere I pleased, and they had faith that I would return home in one piece.

But enter the man who will jolt me from my half sleep. That Saturday on the playground I see a man riding a moped in circles, and at first I barely notice him, though I must have noticed him; otherwise, how can I see him now so clearly in my mind? But I do remember: He smiles pleasantly up at the sky, looks east, then west (imagine Ward Cleaver). His expression is one of a man contemplating another fine day in Southern California as he inhales deeply, closing his eyes, no doubt pondering his good fortune of perpetual sunshine and excellent health. In his Mr. Rogers cardigan, he buzzes around the playground, his moped sputtering, stopping, and then buzzing away again. I see him in the corner of my eye, now in the corner of my memory, noticing that he dismounts his moped to peer at his engine, inspect his tires. I keep pedaling. Nothing about him signals danger. He does not act funny like he's on drugs; he appears to have good grooming habits—a sure sign of stability in my eight-year-old mind.

Then I forget about him. Most likely I'm daydreaming about a crowd of cheering spectators, all of them impressed with my bravery and lightning-speed skills. Over and over, I kick back hard on the pedal, tires screeching to a halt. The applause is ear-splitting! In those moments, I am not a chubby girl with protruding front teeth and a tendency to argue. I am sleek and muscular and pretty with straight white teeth and a racing number taped to my back, and the people rally behind me 100 percent.

Next, another lap around, up a narrow hallway, a quick corner turn, and then: Ward Cleaver appears, no moped, standing smack in the middle of the hallway and completely blocking my path, legs wide apart, larger than life. Moving too fast to change directions, I'm headed straight into him. He's got that same perpetual-sunshine expression as he gazes deeply into my eyes, head tilting to one side—lovingly, almost—reaching out with one hand. It's like one of those mind benders that ask, "What's wrong with this picture?" His pants are unzipped and his belt hangs undone, and he cradles something in his other hand—so gently, so carefully—I think it must be a newborn puppy.

But, what's wrong with this picture?

Swerving away in a reflex, I nearly lose my balance and crash into the wall. Consider, for a moment, the role of chance, of tiny adjustments and minute variations. What if I had crashed into the wall? When are those moments when we jump across the hidden crevasse, sidestepping fissures without even having realized it?

Pedaling home, I ride as fast as I can, though I'm sweaty and burning hot, but not hot with exertion—hot with shame that makes me feel like I've been contaminated by sludge or badness, and I can't tell if it is my badness or his badness, but it's ugly and I won't tell anybody because maybe they'll call me stupid and, besides, I don't want to discuss it.

I imagine what the adults might say. My father: "What the hell, Genius? Why you out there all by yourself?" Or my mother: "Call the police!" Or my father: "Hell with the police.

I'll get my gun." My mother: "And do what?" My father: "Shoot his fucking nuts off, that's what."

So maybe telling the parents wasn't the best idea. In reality, nothing had happened. After all, the man had not touched me. He had only touched himself. Was touching oneself a crime? I did not know. My gut told me it should be, but my parents had not warned me that benign-looking men randomly appear at elementary schools, sometimes dangling their dicks out of their pants. Just not something widely discussed. But I told myself to put my chin up and quit being such a baby. I'm sure I believed, even then, that flashers were ridiculous buffoons, guys who tromped around wearing clown shoes and trench coats—social misfits who made banana jokes and drank margaritas and liked to show people their wieners for a good laugh.

And come on, let's face it—I'd been exposed to worse, hadn't I? Scenes from the R-rated movies that my parents took me to see on Saturday nights left me with images I couldn't forget: decapitated horses' heads, little girls who suddenly cuss in Latin and spit green mucous at priests, and Charles Bronson with his endless supply of bullets, turning bad guys into swiss cheese. I decided not to make a big deal out of it. Also, there was this: maybe I'd done something to deserve it.

II

Years before the playground incident, when I was only three or four, I kept having this dream. The dream would stay with me all day, refusing to evaporate, and all day I would worry about getting killed. The dream would start off with me sitting serenely on the curb in front of our house, sun in my eyes, squinting at the neighborhood children as they play in the street—ghostly silhouettes that jump and shout and twirl. I hear the *swoosh-swoosh* of sprinklers and the *bang-bang* of fathers hammering somewhere, the sputtering up of a lawn mower—all good sounds, safe sounds. After a few moments, though, a fog begins to settle over the neighborhood; kids and the other sounds would fade away, a growing, heavy silence. Then, just as I wonder where everyone has gone, a humped-up black sedan—just like the getaway cars from old gangster movies—glides around the corner, no sound whatsoever coming from its engine. The car gets closer—its whitewall tires rolling gently over asphalt—and then it stops. Right at my feet.

You'd think I could have predicted the outcome after dreaming the same dream forty times, fifty times—even if I was only three or four years old. But dreams are funny that way. Each time, I would sit there on that curb, new and unformed, a child amnesiac happily awaiting my fate. And each time, the plot would unfold in exactly the same sequence: rough hands jerk me off the ground and shove me into a musty, wooden crate. Each time, the same man would loom above me like a cartoon burglar, slamming the lid shut, then the trunk door. Again and again, the same silvery spider webs of light would filter through the cracks—the last light I knew I'd see on this earth. Each time, I gasped for air, kicking the walls of the box with all my might, my scream muffled inside my throat.

The dream would end with the black sedan lurching forward with me in it, for the tenth time, the twentieth time, and then, as if sucked into some cosmic hole, I would feel my body begin to tighten and shrink, compressed by extreme gravity, my very existence reversing itself. Just before disappearing into a single, terrifying sparkle, I would wake up, first in a blinding panic and then gradually comforted to find myself fully formed with skin and toes and ears and hair. Supposedly safe in my bed, my heart would continue to beat for some time like that, like the wings of a desperate hummingbird.

III

My mother liked to tell us tales and we loved to hear them because she always promised us that they were true stories— not made-up ones but real events she'd heard about in the news or something so-and-so had told her at the beauty shop. We learned that in real life good children were not always rescued and that sometimes good children died because of bad luck or strange weather or stupid mistakes, like the little girl crushed by a refrigerator-sized chunk of falling ice or the heroin-addicted mother who dried her baby in the microwave.

When human behavior could not be explained as a stupid mistake or a freak accident, we placed it in the category of "pure evil," as in the case of a man who snatched a sleeping girl from her bed, played with her the way a cat swipes at a cricket, and then buried her alive. My mother told us about the escapades of Charles Manson, a paranoid little man who hyp-notized teenage girls until their eyes went all spirally and then brainwashed them into butchering beautiful starlets. (My mother liked the word *starlet*.) And if you thought family could save you, think again: distraught fathers were always going psycho, including one who set his whole family on fire while they slept (including the dog—what did the dog do?).

But how did any of it make sense to young children? What horrors and dark desires lay in the hearts of men? And was death, then, just a random lottery? Even if I behaved nicely and didn't cuss or steal from my sister's piggy bank, who could say that a light pole would not fall on top of me while I was walk-ing home from school? And knowing all this, shouldn't I go ahead and do whatever I pleased? Still, even with all these questions, the stories seemed spun out of some distant land— not distant in miles but distant in possibility.

By first or second grade, I had amassed a whole arsenal of

such stories—mostly of lost children, dismembered cats, stolen babies—all of them floating through my mind, all of the lost souls in search of their homes. Before school, while I was eating my cold scrambled eggs, I'd study the milk cartons printed with the faces of missing children. "Where are you?" I'd whisper, pretending to have psychic powers. To the freckled boy with ragged bangs: "Send me a sign!" To the teenage girl resembling my babysitter, hair parted down the middle, gap between the teeth: "Don't give up." Closing my eyes, I'd touch a finger to their faces and try to see them. Try to feel what they felt. The ghosts started following me, or so I thought, or maybe I started following the ghosts. Somehow, I felt that our lives had become connected, intertwined. I let myself love them. Who else would remember them? Where were their bodies now? Curled up in some musty old crate? Hidden beneath a pile of decaying leaves, fast-motion worms nibbling at their flesh?

And why did the killers get all the attention? Other criminals would remain beneath the radar, safely hidden away in bushes and school yards, sometimes wearing their "nice guy" disguises. Who would notice these men who did not actually kill children but wanted only to possess them for brief seconds, giving these children a part of themselves, like some bizarre birthday present? How were children to behave, then, and what recourse did they have, unaware of this weird middle land?

IV

Two girls, your age, disappear from a bus stop. It's November 1977, and the people in the city are in a panic. Young women start turning up dead near the freeways of Glendale and northern Los Angeles. Their bodies, luminous and pale, have been laid out like museum displays across garbage-littered scrub grass and natty hillsides.

Meanwhile, you are eleven going on twelve. You listen to *Frampton Comes Alive*, your very first real album. On your baby record player the music crackles and skips, but who cares, it's the first music that belongs to you—not your mother's Liza Minnelli show tunes or the *Saturday Night Fever* soundtrack, to which you now declare: Disco Sucks!

Peter Frampton, a skinny guy with haunted eyes, eases the pain of sixth grade, which bores you to death. Your teacher, Mr. Stuebner, talks mostly about dirt bikes and motorcycles and the foot-long metal pin in his arm. Then, when he runs out of dirt-bike stories, he turns on the classroom's television set and dozes off in the back of the room, arms crossed, snoring. You sleep too, waking up with a puddle of drool beneath your cheek. Three of your classmates laugh at you as you try to wipe it up. But this is your life. Key word: *alive*.

Those days you walk home from school alone, like most kids. There is no such thing as a Child Drop-Off Line or a Child Pickup Line, and parents do not have to sign permission slips and contracts every five seconds. In those days, once the three o'clock bell rings, the school doors open, and kids pour out into the smoggy afternoon, scattering every which way. A few stragglers linger at school until teachers shoo them off; others loiter across the street in front of the market, dropping Pop Rocks on their tongues and skidding off the curb with their skateboards, but every night they arrive home safely.

It's an easy eight-block stroll through a middle-class, tree-lined neighborhood; the sun burns bright but the shade feels cool, and you have survived another day of clock watching with Mr. Stuebner. It's all downhill after three o'clock. There you go, meandering down Hermosa Street, inhaling deeply of the orange haze, humming, and taking your sweet time. In spots where the sidewalk recedes into shade beside blooming camellias and man-sized Japanese ferns, you pause to fan the back of your neck, shivering as the sweat rolls down your back and dries. Still only half-aware, you notice a van parked alongside the curb where there isn't usually a van. Vans could be so groovy then—remember? Wall-to-wall carpeting, porthole bubble windows, chain-link steering wheels. Love Mobiles. This van, though, scraped with rough blue primer, no windows—strictly for transport—isn't groovy. Who would notice it? After all, this is a street, and cars are supposed to park on streets, right?

So here you are, an eleven-year-old girl with a frizzy home perm and braces with tiny pink rubber bands connecting top incisors to bottom incisors. Most likely you're wearing one of your baggy made-in-India blouses with the snaky embroidery across the chest. (You wear a B-cup bra already, and your attitude toward your developing breasts is a confusing mix of pride and horror.)

But here is the van. Then the side door slides open. (Haven't you learned anything?)

(Birds sing.)

You are ten feet away.

(An airplane buzzes overhead.)

You are five feet away.

(A mourning dove coos.)

At the very least, admit your curiosity. Hitching the strap of your backpack higher, you keep walking, edging toward the fence. In that van you expect to see paint cans, tools, other equipment, a couple of paint-splattered guys hauling a bucket or a ladder.

But here is what you get: a naked man on his knees, masturbating like crazy, frenzied, his whole hairy body flexing and thrusting into his hand, flat, black eyes staring. He'd been waiting for you. No flasher jokes now.

"Come 'ere," he says, breathing hard, his head thrown back. His face, like a branding iron, burns into your memory in a single flash. Do you imagine the desperate, dark air that emits from the van—air that reeks of despair, of struggle? Do you imagine the deep, low thrum that resonates from the van, a sound that only you can hear? Don't think though. Run, now. Pretend you are a track star! Listen how the audience cheers you on. Run as fast as you can

Linda, your nine-year-old sister, has beaten you home. Burning hot and out of breath, you slam the door, shrug off the backpack, and run to the window.

"Oh shit, oh shit, oh shit," you mutter, crouching down and scoping. "Did you see him? Did you see that guy?"

"What guy? What are you talking about?" she says.

Dragging the curtains across the window, you tell your little sister about the pervert in the van. Your mother has told you about all the dead girls because their smiling school portraits are all plastered over the *LA Times*, but what does this have to do with you? Still, you race to lock all the doors. Your sister, even on the verge of hysterics, thinks fast—she picks up the phone, dials the operator, and repeats the story: naked man, van, sister.

"What are you doing?" you shriek-whisper. (Good luck wrestling the receiver away from her; she's strong.) She hisses, "What if he followed you, *stupid*? What if he knows where you live?" Of course, she's right. You're not thinking about tomorrow or other girls or this guy's next move. You are thinking about YOU, and wondering what you've done to deserve this (boohoo) and what invisible signals your body is sending out behind your back. Think of your dog Cleo when she goes into heat and how stray mongrels come panting at the gate, hell-bent on getting in the yard, and how a part of you despises poor Cleo as she sits panting on the patio, looking up, down, biting at a flea, oblivious, and now how you despise yourself because you can't stop your boobs from growing no matter how many melba toasts you eat for dinner or how many hundreds of laps you swim. You can think all you want, but don't even try to connect the pieces. Not yet. You'd best just wait it out, crouching beneath the window—no adults needed, thank you very much. You'd just as soon never mention this again and go along your merry way, even though you feel naked and you'll start wearing sweaters every single day regardless of the temperature, buttoned right up to the neck.

Minutes later police cars and a black sedan pull up in front of the house. Suddenly you hear walkie-talkies beeping, heavy footsteps, men's voices. Why so many cops? Why the fuss? Peeking out from behind the curtains you glimpse the edges of uniforms, starched navy fabric, gleaming badges, guns, solid and heavy in their holsters. These are the good guys, so you open the door. They sit you and Linda down on the couch, bombarding you with questions as they scribble into their notepads, pausing intermittently to mumble into their radios. One man, dressed in polyester pants and a chunky striped tie, shakes your hand and says, "Hi, kiddo, I'm Detective Goodman, and I'll be handing your case."

Case? Then your mother arrives home, all flushed and flabbergasted, scared that they'll arrest her for leaving you alone. The detectives don't give a damn about that. The good guys are on your side. They tell you and your mother to meet them at the station, *pronto*, to sit with their sketch artist so you can make a picture of this creep while he's fresh in your memory.

In the car: "Thanks a lot," you mumble ungratefully to the little sister. Her blotchy face is streaked with tears. "That man could have killed you," she insists, sniffling. She's mad at you.

Your mother scolds, "Be glad someone around here has some sense."

"How is this even my fault?" you whine, feeling all persecuted, and they say, "You should be more scared. This is not a joke."

At the station, a nervous detective asks you many questions about penises, pantomiming with his hands. "Okay, honey, was this man's, uh . . . PENIS . . . uh, erect or not erect, okay . . . in other words, uh . . . was it standing up or, uh, laying down?" He wants to know about the shape of the penis. He wants to know if you understand the difference between circumcised and not circumcised. After that, the sketch artist, armed with charcoal pencils and a white pad, ekes out a fair likeness of the man's face. In the end, the picture looks accurate to you—soulless, empty as a mannequin, and a little bit like Starsky from *Starsky & Hutch*.

V

Haven't you learned of any obvious signs? You are seventeen years old and you go jogging in the middle of the day. (Yes, you know what's coming.) A shaggy-haired Sasquatch leaps out of the bushes, coming at you with his pants down, wielding his penis like it's a lightsaber. But maybe you *have* learned a lesson: If the good guys have taught you anything, they have taught you that you are not a dumb robot. You are not a dirty girl. You are not as powerful as you thought either. Things happen with or without you. So. You march straight to the police department, still wearing your running clothes, still sweating. "I want to make a report," you say, out of breath. The detective, a woman, sits you right down. "I'm a detective and I'll be handling this case," she says, holding out her hand. It is strong and her fingers are warm. You describe the man without the slightest trace of embarrassment. You now know words for each body part—you keep a copy of *Gray's Anatomy* on your desk and you got an A in biology. You point easily to his face in a photo album filled with other criminals. A week later the detective calls you up to thank you and to tell you that they arrested that creep and that he won't be bothering you anytime soon.

Postscript to IV

Fast-forward: You are thirtysomething, lounging around and thumbing through the pages of a dog-eared paperback, a book about the Los Angeles Hillside Stranglers, one that you found at some used bookstore, a made-for-TV book about two cousins and their month-long killing spree. Flipping right to the good part—the photos—you see a single picture that makes you forget, suddenly, who you are and what you are doing. The ground tilts.

Where do I know this person from? you'll ask yourself. Those flat eyes, the hardened jaw, the branding iron to the memory, your birthday present.

Of course, you'll need proof. Do the research, check the dates, examine the evidence. But you were there, that November, walking free, listening to Peter Frampton. Forget the stupid jokes you'll want tell your future children, like, "Your mama is SO ugly, the serial killer left her on the curb!"

Stop looking at his picture now—enough of him. Instead, study the faces of the girls from that November, girls who listened to Led Zeppelin and maybe hated (or loved) the sixth grade, girls who wore Love's Baby Soft perfume and kept Strawberry Lip Smackers stashed in their pockets. Understand that all their light was sucked into a black vortex. Surprise, surprise, one girl looks like you—a sixth-grader with brown hair, metal barrettes, half smile. Imagine her fate, jerked off her feet, pushed into a trunk . . . but then stop there. Don't dwell on the ending. Imagine instead the beginning, the middle. Understand that death does not define her. Nor does it define any of them. Now think about you. Was it luck? Was it smarts? How did you sidestep the crevasse? All you can know is this: you are still here. Key word: *alive*. Look up at the sky. You are fully formed: skin and toes, ears and hair.

VI

These days, I study the FBI's mile-long missing-persons list, trying to honor those faces, those stories, reading about the circumstances in which they disappeared, hoping they'll send me a clue. As for their fate, four real possibilities exist:

1. They fell into a ditch and wedged a head or ankle between two boulders.
2. They got beamed up by aliens (hopefully kind, intelligent, wide-eyed aliens like the ones in *Close Encounters of the Third Kind*).
3. They are living under an alias, happily ever after, on a tropical island.
4. You know the other possibility.

As for my own children, I have to warn them about these things, that people can be damaged in ways that I cannot explain with words. I teach them about kidnappers and perverts: Do I have a choice? My children learned words in this order: *Mama, Papa, Sun, Moon, Kidnapper*. Our front porch is not called a porch but a safety zone, though of course I realize that safety is nothing but an illusion. I tell them about bad guys and good guys, but then comes the gray area. Can a bad guy ever be a girl? Can a person who looks like a bad guy actually be a good guy? Can a person who looks like a good guy actually be a bad guy? Can a good guy ever do a bad thing and still be a good guy? Yes, yes, yes, and maybe, I answer, only to be met with blank stares. I show my children the website. We find our map and click on the bubble nearest our house—behind our house. A smiling middle-aged man appears on the page. His photo captures an expression as though he's just heard a joke and he's about to beat us to the punch line. "Study his face," I tell my children, and we do, as though we are looking at an insect through the lens of a microscope.

The Burrito

A BRIEF HISTORY

A burrito, historically, was a food of convenience, much like the sandwich, a transport vehicle for the meal itself—beans, shredded meat, vegetables, or whatever ingredients one had on hand. The large flour tortilla, however, is an American creation equivalent to soft white bread and often preferred over the yellow-corn "peasant" tortilla because of its size, thus making it both more filling and more portable. The burrito, traditionally the food of workers, can be quickly rolled and wrapped in paper and easily stashed—convenient for the fields or the factory, no spoon or fork required. The tortilla, when torn into pieces, functions as a "poor man's fork," and when rolled into burrito form becomes the fork, the plate, and the napkin.

My mother recalls eating her lunch in the school bathroom, always feeling ashamed of food that looked and smelled so ethnic. Plus, she felt that her lunch looked ugly compared to those of the other children, with their pretty red apple slices and peanut butter and jelly sandwiches minus the brown crusts. Her lunch: a misshapen oval of flat bread with charcoal spots, rolled and filled with a hodgepodge of leftovers: pinto beans, bits of scrambled egg, shredded meat, strips of jack cheese (and whatever else was available). How she longed for an all-American Oscar Mayer bologna sandwich on Weber's white bread with swirls of Hellmann's mayonnaise and a handful of Lay's potato chips laid carefully atop the bologna and squeezed flat between the bread until the chips crushed like the bones of a little bird.

––––––

"Burrito" means small donkey, but a burrito (the food) does not resemble a donkey, so perhaps the burrito itself—a roll, a cylinder—resembles packs that burros carry. Burros are work animals that carry loads down narrow dusty paths, up mountain trails, across deserts; though they may be tired, they do not (normally) complain. Flies walk across their eyeballs, and they allow it to happen, gently swishing their tails in mild protest. Biologists believe that the first donkeys were brought to the Americas by Christopher Columbus on his second voyage, first to Hispaniola and later to North America to aid enslaved Natives.

––––––

The American culinary world now embraces the burrito and dresses it up with more respectable fillings. They've ditched the refried beans and melted cheese but kept the form and the basic concept, the insides now being filled with various multicultural ingredients. Consider the many modern fillings: curried lentils; cashews and swiss chard; miso paste and sea scallops; quinoa and adzuki beans. One may now eat wraps or roll-ups, which come in festive colors like green or red and can be sliced at artful angles to reveal the beauty of the layered fillings. Such burritos are not to be eaten on the go but with knives and forks inside upscale restaurants—places with subdued lighting and cloth napkins, slices of lemon in the water. In contrast to the upscale burrito, the fast-food burrito has become an everyday affair, stuffed with scrambled eggs and hush puppies, American-cheese triangles, pork sausage, strips of bacon, and even french fries. One fast-food restaurant sells a burrito that contains a tostada, which would be like eating a hamburger with an entire hot dog between the buns or a hot dog with a piece of pizza next to the weenie.

———

My mother worked long days. Too tired to make dinner, she'd buy us burritos, which we ate in the car on our way home from school or on errands. Pedro's Place made the best burritos— distinctive because of a fragrant tomatillo-pork green sauce made by the family's grandma, who wore a pink checkered apron and could be seen through a little window always stir- ring the contents of a boiling vat or up to her elbows in a bowl of masa. One bite of the grandma's green pork burrito felt like a tiny trip to heaven, no plates needed. We'd eat our dinner inside the Dodge van while my mother ran into the Alpha Beta or Lucky Supermarket to get some milk or some diapers. Little sister in her car seat. Brothers licking beans that have dribbled down their arms. All of us cradling our warm burritos in our palms as if it's our last meal on earth.

———

Eating a burrito requires faith, for what's inside is naturally concealed by the cylindrical structure. You take your chances when you bite into a tortilla that is clearly stuffed with something, the contents being a mystery until you have the whole thing in your mouth.

One time my brother-in-law (who happens to be a white guy from the Midwest and did not grow up eating burritos) took a bite and felt a gentle crunch between his teeth: a popping sensation, gristle on the tongue, and then an alarming bitter taste. When he spat it out and poked around at the thing with his fork, he discovered that he had in fact bitten into a cockroach—now slimy and boiled flat, and of course partially chewed. This incident, not surprisingly, made him wary of all burritos for a very long time.

And because burritos conceal their contents, they are excellent for playing tricks and getting revenge. My mother and father employed about ten men—a ragtag crew of electricians and refrigerator-repair guys, who after work would lean against the hoods of the company trucks drinking beer and complaining, often one-upping each other with stories meant to illustrate another electrician's unbelievable stupidity. In the grimy repair-yard bathroom, a mystery employee—an artist—would take time to sketch anatomically detailed pictures of naked ladies wearing come-hither expressions, their legs spread wide, their enormous boobs practically eclipsing their faces. My mother never seemed particularly bothered by this "poor-man's porn," but she did mention that one of these jerks had been stealing her lunch.

My mother would bring her lunch and place it in the office refrigerator, and each day her lunch would disappear. Finally she decided to get her revenge. She brought a decoy lunch—a burrito with something concealed inside. She later confessed how she'd scouted out and collected the contents—horror of horrors—a mound of fresh dog shit produced by our beloved

Cleo. She explained how preparing it had made her gag and that she thought she'd surely burn in hell, but she'd managed to roll out the decoy just like a normal burrito. She wrapped it in foil and placed it on a paper plate with a little packet of taco sauce to make it look extra enticing. When her lunch disappeared that day, she thought it was the funniest thing that had ever happened. I, on the other hand, could not help but think about the mystery man. How many bites did he take before he realized what was inside? What if, by some miracle, he ate the whole thing and never even realized what he'd eaten? What if he got so sick that he had to be hospitalized? Would he ever have faith in a burrito again?

———

Sometimes on Sundays we would eat our burritos inside a little restaurant we called the Car Wash—a tiny café that had no other name that I can remember. We called it the Car Wash because the restaurant was directly next to the Mission Car Wash, where my mother would sometimes get her car washed and vacuumed. The beans there were not rolled up in a tortilla but ladled onto a salad plate and sprinkled with jack cheese. The waitress with the bleached orange hair and silver tooth would bring endless baskets of warm, speckled tortillas, and as soon as one plate of beans had been eaten, another would appear. The beans, so delectable, did not even need a tortilla, so sometimes we would revert to the spoon—a stainless-steel bean platform, one might say—all the focus on the beans themselves, no embellishment needed. Through the restaurant's window we could watch the workers polishing hubcaps and spraying windshields with squirt bottles that hooked on to their belts. They'd honk the cars' horns and wave their dirty rags at the cars' owners, who would hurry over to claim their sparkling vehicles. Sometimes customers would give the workers a dollar. Other times the customers would just nod and snatch their car keys. An endless stream of cars moved through that lot. Those workers kept drying and polishing, and we kept eating. On those Sundays, we thought about what we wanted to be when we grew up and we thought about school and we thought about our friends and our mother and our father and our teachers and sometimes it seemed like we spent our whole lives sitting there, watching those guys and eating our beans. You felt like you could never get enough then, and you'd ask for another plate, and then another, and the woman with the silver tooth would just smile and nod.

An Elegy (and Apology) to Dogs I've Loved

> Here they are. The soft eyes open.
> If they have lived in a wood
> It is a wood.
> If they have lived on plains
> It is grass rolling
> Under their feet forever.
> —from "The Heaven of Animals" by JAMES DICKEY

Taco

In the photograph, I'm three years old and wearing a white lace–eyelet Easter dress and matching gloves. I'm poking my gloved finger through the chain-link fence of our driveway, while you, a wispy black-and-white mutt, whine behind that fence—the same fence through which you will eventually disappear into a maze of alleys and side streets, most likely skittering away from speeding trucks and strangers who will spook you with their outstretched hands.

I cannot remember missing you. I cannot remember loving you. I am sorry for that. What did I know? After all, a three-year-old human and a dog have this in common: they watch and wait, wondering if the sun will fall from the sky. That year an earthquake shook our house, and I remember my father grabbing me from my bed as dishes toppled from cabinets and the television set jumped across the room. Without fear, I stared at the walls, waiting for them to crack apart, just as you had probably stared at the dirt, head cocked, waiting for the earth to split open. If I remember being three, I remember being a dog, for in my family, one became the other. How good it felt, then, lying outside with you, our bellies pressed against cool concrete, sow bugs wriggling under our noses amid silt and burned leaves, the unpredictable sun burning right through our fur.

Sandy

Crouched on my knees in the gutter of Hermosa Avenue, I'm stroking your silky, red fur, seeing you through a blur of tears, morning sunlight through water, shards of soft glass, fractals. Someone has carried you here to the side of the road, and now blood runs from your muzzle and drips onto the concrete. Your blood, brighter than I'd imagined, soaks into a shred of newspaper that someone has placed against your nose. Adults hover over me now, citizens moved by this pathetic scene of a little girl and her dead dog. Cars swoosh by, the wind from the tires blowing my hair, rippling your fur. Come on now, they say, catching me under the armpits and trying to lift me up. *Where do you live?* And I keep saying, "Somebody left the gate open."

To you: *I* probably left the gate open, and I am sorry. A wish: I hope it felt good to run free, even if only for a few minutes, right before that metal beast came smashing into you.

Tiger

My darling, Tiger, I am learning about the folly of men. I am stroking your nose, watching you squint against the sun, and I want to keep you here forever, gentle Tiger. Some men do not believe in the souls of animals, perhaps because they do not believe in the souls of themselves. I am sorry that I did not stop him, that bricklayer man working in our backyard who wanted to amuse me by hurling you into the sky, who laughed his head off as he flung you up and then barely caught you as you sailed into his rough, brown hands. I still see his cement-streaked face and your reflection in his sunglasses—your legs askew, eyes bulging with terror. I am sorry that my tongue froze that day. Since then, I have learned to speak up, and I think you would be proud (if dogs can be proud). I once saw a man pounding his dog with his fist and I told him, "How about punching someone your own size, you loser?" and he said, "Shut up, bitch, before I punch you," and I said, "Oh, please do, be my guest."

Why are we humans so slow to learn? One version of heaven would be if we could go back in time and revise the flawed scenes of our lives. I should have bitten the bricklayer's leg or thrown rocks at him. I have lived with this regret. The next day, when you disappeared, I understood why. I wanted to leave too, for what creature with any sense would remain in such a place?

C. P. O. Sharkey

First of all, sorry about the name.

You arrived in the age of television: my younger brothers named you after a short-lived sitcom in which Don Rickles played Chief Petty Officer Sharkey, a cantankerous old bigot who insulted people left and right. You might have just as easily been named Gomer Pyle, Gilligan, or the Six Million Dollar Dog, but what do young boys raised by television know of heroes?

When he'd brought you home, my father thought he'd

found a dog to match his own manliness—a dog of the Third Reich, no less, of Adolf Hitler himself. For a few days, my father took an interest in you—throwing a ball, calling you "boy," scratching your ears, while my brothers ran alongside, happy for not only one but two male role models. When my father lost interest in you, everything fell apart. My father obviously did not know that even Adolf Hitler, between his acts of unspeakable horrors, had employed a full-time dog handler for his beloved Blondi, and that German shepherds, like boys, require a pack leader, training, a firm hand.

Imprisoned in our backyard with its swimming pool and patch of lawn, you turned rogue, went out of control, looking at us quizzically and then peering hard at our faces for some word of direction, no other solution but to tear apart a rhododendron, dig a hole, gnash your teeth against the wrought-iron gate. While you yipped and yelped, knocked people down, and destroyed furniture, my seven- and eight-year-old brothers got sent to the principal's office for using words like *fucker* and *retard* and for trying to light fires in the bathroom trash can. The brothers, with the right training, might have been baseball stars or engineers. You might have been a police dog or a cadaver dog with medals dangling from your collar and "The Star Spangled Banner" filling your ears.

As for me, I am sorry that I kicked you. I am sorry that I hated you when you chewed on my ankle with your shark-sharp teeth and nudged my face with your muzzle, slopping your big grassy tongue across my teeth. I regret not buying a book and training you myself. I regret the times I locked myself in my bedroom and refused to throw a tennis ball to you, to my brothers. I am learning that for kids and dogs both, life is a tricky proportion of fate and free will. We live with what we've got, often at our peril.

But of all things, I am sorry for my mother, who coaxed you into the car with that weenie and drove you to the mountains and abandoned you there. She says she couldn't take it anymore. She says she never wanted a dog in the first place. She said my father was always bringing animals home and dumping them on us. Understand that unlike dogs, humans connive and cower, that their backbones, like their loyalty, always weakens. Walking upright takes its toll. For years I've imagined you watching the car as it drove away, you with your ears perked and your head tilted, looking perplexed and wondering why the human had not thrown the ball, wondering where cars go when they shrink out of sight. I see you trotting off into the wilderness, saved by instinct as you follow the hot scent of a jackrabbit, then dart after it into the woods.

I have prayed that in that wilderness you swiftly forgot us (and your name) and found a human with a strong backbone, one who taught you to sit and stay and lie down, and that over the span of your lifetime, you caught a million Frisbees and an abundance of fat trout in your happy, slobbering jaws.

Petunia

You, Petunia, were the product of a broken home. Here's a little tip about humans: unlike dogs, we cannot live long in packs. We pair-bond, like mallards, but then abandon our mates, too mired are we in a muck of emotions, too intelligent about our own mortality and obsessed, therefore, with youth and revenge and pride. You lived in the mansion in the foothills built by my parents right before their divorce. My father moved to an apartment with another woman, my mother filed for divorce, and our unfinished mansion sat atop the hill like a dead horse. The perimeter of the property remained wide open—all those curtainless windows, all those unlockable doors—the yard craggy and cratered like the surface of the moon. Any of us could have disappeared, then, I suppose. It's a wonder we lost only you.

Now I see your ghost sometimes on canyon trails, under shrubs. When I think of you, I think of the two of us home alone in that big house on Christmas Eve, me in bed, miserable with the flu and feeling sorry for myself, you curled at my feet, and a big knife stashed under the mattress for our protection. Sometimes I see you at the end of the road that led down to the glen—you walking the dog (yourself), sniffing gently the edges of ivy, of baby oaks. The mountain lion lowers his head, his eyes luminescent as he springs forth and sinks his fangs into your neck, easily pinning you beneath his feline heft.

We fell apart; *things fall apart,* and later I would always associate Yeats's words with this time: *The blood-dimmed tide is loosed, and everywhere / The ceremony of innocence is drowned.* I hope the lion made good use of you, flesh into flesh, muscle into muscle. That part is fate. I am sorry about the unfinished fences, the faithlessness of humans, and bad endings. That part is free will.

Spicy

On the green leather couch, your belly practically bursts with unborn pups that I can feel wriggling beneath the tight drum of your skin. I am sixteen, lost and anonymous in a new high school, having not yet made friends who understand my jokes. Your calm body steadies me, then, as we doze in slants of sunlight amid sparkles of dust.

The day the puppies are born, I pretend to be your midwife, with a stack of towels at my side, a boiled set of tongs in my hands (for what?), crouching next to you inside that refrigerator box that I'd cut with an X-ACTO knife and lined with newspaper, urging you, "Come on, girl, you can do it!" You play along with my ridiculous charade, looking at me mindlessly, panting and panting and panting. Suddenly you go silent as your muscles contract and you hold your breath: a pup emerges, unmoving and slick in its membrane. How do you know to furiously lick this small creature and to quickly chomp away the umbilical sac, devouring that strange flesh in a single swallow? How do you know to nudge at the pup until it mews and kicks, its insistent pale tongue already in search of a nipple? One pup after another emerges from your body, until— thirteen pups? I repeat: thirteen pups? How good you were to lie there as they pawed at you and gummed you and scratched your belly raw. How patient; how devoted! A model of true motherhood! So many years later, when I nursed my own baby, dead tired and again feeling sorry for myself, I would see you in that box and imagine myself imbued with a fraction of your mother instinct.

Over the years I will not tell your story, because people will give me "the look," and in their eyes I will see reflected all the lost and unwanted dogs in the world, all the shelters filled with unwanted animals, all the lethal injections and piles of discarded bodies. I am sorry about how you later sniffed in drawers, in closets, forlorn and unsettled, as human after human came to take away your offspring. I am so sorry if any of your offspring came to a bad end, imprisoned at the end of a chain, kicked, or hungry. But I cannot be sorry about the beauty of that day—the miracle, my God!—not for one second am I sorry for that day of new life with its smell of blood and wet newspapers.

Caesar

> I had rather be a dog, and bay the moon,
> Than such a Roman.
> —*Julius Caesar*

So rather than define you by how you died (in the jaws of Coco the Rottweiler; you chased him down), I will define you by the submarine sandwich from Claro's Italian Deli that you once snatched from me.

"Give it to me," I said.

"Drop it," I commanded.

You growled—first low and quiet, and then louder as I approached.

Grabbing the edge of the plastic-wrapped sandwich, I said, "Give it to me," and yanked hard. You clenched your jaws tighter, the edges of your lips curling as you bared your teeth. Then you took two quick gobbles closer to my hand, and I saw the whites of your eyes.

I surrendered. The sandwich was yours. For the rest of my life, I will not forget that moldy thing and your loyalty to it, even above your loyalty to me, whom I believe you loved more than anyone else. I have admired you for your self-control and how you never actually ate it but only admired it. How carefully you would retrieve that putrid prize from its hiding place, carrying it to a spot in the sun, where you would lounge on your belly, your hind legs splayed as you gently licked the plastic wrapper, softly gnawing the edge of it and languishing in your fragrant salami, ham, and provolone reverie.

I will not apologize to you, for more than the others, you took what you wanted, died as you pleased.

Max

Searching for you led me to places I wouldn't normally go.

That night, trudging through alleys, I tripped over dented cans, used syringes, stray tires, and my own shoelaces. I walked and walked until I reached the edges of the freeway—a wasteland of rusted-out car parts and tumbleweeds.

Against backyards, chain-link fences, across the highways, I searched, desperate for you, finding only these humpbacked creatures that darted here and there. Mute as pharaohs, they flashed their obsidian eyes, offering me nothing, offended that I'd intruded into their nightly rites of love and sacrifice.

Gripping my flashlight at 2 a.m., I marched right up to some porch where two cholos were kicking back and drinking malt liquor. They watched me approach, their heads back, feet up on the rail, smirking, and probably surprised, then, by their own sentimentality. They softened up and said softly, "Little dog?" and, "No, nah, we ain't seen no dog." Leaning forward on their elbows, they peered into the darkness, this way, that way. "Man, that sucks," one said softly. "We'll keep an eye out," the other offered, standing up, not knowing what to do next.

For some weird reason I wanted to tell those guys your whole story, about how after fourteen years you'd finally grown rheumy and senile, about all the bits of scrambled eggs and rice I'd pushed into your toothless mouth, about how you'd get stuck up against a wall, frozen in time, until I'd nudge you with my foot, reminding you to live, and that now you'd wandered out the gate and turned into a phantom.

Here is a confession: I loved my own child more than I loved you. Distracted by motherhood, I lost keys, left gates open, misplaced my wallet at least fifty times. Even as I searched for you those nights with my Lost Dog flyers in hand, I prayed that I would never lose my child. Let this be a lesson, I thought, imagining my daughter safe in her crib. *Thank God, I've only lost the dog*, I thought, imagining the parents of never-to-be-found children, their eternity of searching.

All your incessant barking! Mindless pacing! Growling at every damned sound ever known to man. I am sorry that in exchange for those years of loyal service, your end came in a flood of blinding headlights—the driver no doubt mistaking the gentle crush of your old bones for a brittle tree branch. Please know, if you can know at all, that in the dark, I too have stumbled across blackened puddles in search of my devotions, regretting every unlatched gate, and for you, old friend, cursing every single cat that ever lived.

Nine Days of Ruth

I

The day Grandma Ruth began to die, a blue jay came knocking at my mother's front door. We watched him through the front window as he hopped up the steps and across the porch, where he squawked as if to announce his arrival. Then he began pecking earnestly at the baseboard, no apparent purpose other than the pecking itself. Clearly, he had a job to do, and nothing was going to stop him. That whole morning my mother had assumed that some hooligan was playing doorbell ditch. Finally, she spied the true culprit: the jay tilted his head, surveyed the scene with a beady black eye, and then resumed knocking—a rhythmic *tat-tat-tat*. In my family, a bird on a windowsill or inside a house signifies impending death—nature's heads-up—a tiny escort come to usher the spirit to the underworld. So we let him knock, tried to stay out of his way.

When I had arrived that morning, a saint candle was burning on the nightstand, the dim light illuminating framed photographs of grandchildren and Ruth's ceramic frogs, some wearing vaudeville hats or little tuxedos—others wearing sunglasses and dopey expressions—all of them in various poses throughout the room. Now the room smells different—swampy almost, like soil rolling itself under, like leaves moldering beneath other leaves—ironic, considering the frogs.

I press my palm against her forehead because that is what you must do when someone is dying; that is, touch her, hold her steady, and keep her well anchored until she drifts off— choose your metaphor. Her skin feels like the surface of a mushroom (amphibious perhaps), and I wonder if decomposition has already begun. Many doctors will tell you that death cannot be defined in a single moment, though the official pronouncement will be made after the final heartbeat. Still, the body dies in stages—organ by organ—and I wonder about the skin, the shroud that surrounds the other organs.

Autolysis, meaning "self-digestion," occurs when the cells' lysosomes release digestive enzymes into the cytoplasm, whereupon the cells begin to digest themselves; thus the body begins the recycling process. Such beauty, even in reverse! Imagine a person, beginning with the zygote—see the golden cell cluster that pushes into a shape like a salamander. See the tail, webbed feet; notice the creature unfurling itself like a fern—how finally it pushes itself, by some miracle, into a human creature. If all goes well, the creature's brain will grow *inside* the skull, the heart *inside* the ribs, and the creature develops ten fingers and ten toes, no more webbing, no more tail. See the creature expelled from the womb. Watch it grow upright, run, eat, digest, breathe, pump, secrete. Watch how the creature merges with another creature—a spark! A new zygote forms, and then another, and another, and another. Consider the years of biological success. Finally, hear the distress signal—a siren from the brain. *All hands on deck! Fire in the hole! SOS!* Abandon ship. Autolysis has begun.

II

When you sit with a dying person, you start thinking about the strangest things. The mind wanders, searching for another puzzle, another problem. I start thinking about the story I'd once heard about an elderly woman who lived in a nursing home. One morning, when the nursing aides arrived to dress her, they were horrified to find the old woman covered with a layer of tiny black ants. The ants had already begun colonizing, organizing themselves into a road map across her body. Apparently, the ants had trailed in from the garden through the gap under the door, marched across the room and up the bedpost, traversed the sheets up onto her fingers, and then crawled inside the sleeve of her nightgown (final destination unknown). The nurses could not explain it! The old woman had not stashed a cookie in her pocket; nor was she sick or dying (at least not visibly). By the time her eyelids fluttered open, she never knew that a thousand little creatures had tried to stake their claim. Though she appeared healthy, she ended up dying soon after. So, somehow, the ants had come too soon. Or had they? Was it a problem with timing, or did the ants know more than the humans? Did nature sometimes make mistakes? And was this even an act of nature? And who even knew the difference?

Another thought: Sitting with a dying person turns you into a voyeur. You gaze at the body and try to etch certain features into your mind—those traits you most want to remember— knobby knees and strong white teeth, still good for another hundred years. Of course, had my grandmother been conscious, I might not have touched her with a lingering hand or scrutinized her so steadily, for such physical intimacy would have certainly embarrassed us both.

But this is how it's supposed to be, I think. This is not a child dying from leukemia, like Casey Aceves, Ruth's grandson who died at age fifteen. Nor is this a child drowned in a mud hole, like Ruth's little brother, who died at age three. Ruth's death is not a tragedy! Here, rather, is a ninety-three-year-old woman who's come full circle: seven children, all alive, and sixty-five grandchildren (all alive minus Casey, *RIP*)—an explosion of life, of lives, more on the way. Charles Darwin might say that, in the end, Ruth had adapted superbly to her environment and that in the meantime she'd managed to pass on some resilient genes.

The hospice nurse arrives and places the stethoscope against Ruth's chest, listening to her breath. He places two fingers on her wrist and looks at his watch. Then he adjusts her head, writes some notes on a clipboard, and says, "Oh, yes, she's slipping away; she might pass any time now."

This delicate language gets me thinking about death euphemisms, which makes me wonder what Ruth would have to say about Monty Python's dead parrot sketch. Man walks into a pet shop to return his dead bird. Clerk insists that the bird is not dead—just *restin'* and *pinin' for the fjords*.

"No, no!" Mr. Praline, the bird owner, says, insisting that the bird is dead. Finally Mr. Praline declares in frustration:

'E's not pinin'! 'E's passed on! This parrot is no more! He has ceased to be! 'E's expired and gone to meet 'is maker! 'E's a stiff! Bereft of life, 'e rests in peace! If you hadn't nailed 'im to the perch 'e'd be pushing up the daisies! 'Is metabolic processes are now 'istory! 'E's off the twig! 'E's kicked the bucket, 'e's shuffled off 'is mortal coil, run down the curtain and joined the bleedin' choir invisible!! THIS IS AN EX-PARROT!!

I want to talk to Grandma Ruth about the language, tell her

that she's knocking at death's door, about to croak (think frogs), about to kick the bucket, and that soon she'll be six feet under in the boneyard, gone to meet her maker, food for the worms, an *ex-grandma*, rest in peace. I think she'd laugh.

(But I could be wrong.)

Meanwhile, the blue jay keeps knocking.

III

On the third day, relatives start showing up—long-lost cousins, out-of-townies, and even my best friend, Dana, whom Grandma had claimed long ago as another grandchild. Outside, our children run in arcs around Grandma's window, repelled, almost, by the room itself. Some force seems to be pushing them in the opposite direction. A silent voice seems to command: "Run! Play! Escape while you can!"

I don't want my children to think of death as scary or unnatural, but let's be honest—it is scary!—the raspy breathing, the contracting muscles, the half-opened eyes. So I try to keep explanations simple and realistic: I tell my two-year-old son that Grandma Ruth's body is old and tired and that her heart will soon stop beating and then her body will stop working forever. But try explaining death to a two-year-old. Our discussion goes something like this:

"Where will she go?"

"After she dies, we'll put her body in a box and bury the box in a hole," I say.

"Will she turn into a skeleton?"

"Yes."

"Will she climb out of the hole and rattle her bones around?"

"No."

"Won't she be scared under the ground?"

"No, because her body won't have feelings."

"Why?"

"'Cause she'll be dead, Buddy."

"Will I be dead?

[Pause] "Yes, but not for a *really* long time."

"Will you be dead?"

"Yes, but not until you grow up and become a man. [Another pause] Oh hey, look! I see a ball! Wanna kick the ball?"

Then I kiss-kiss-kiss his salty head, grab his sticky hands, and, with all my might, give him a helicopter twirl. Time and gravity press down upon us, and it hits me then how fast it's all moving, how quickly we're running in place on a spinning earth. One day I'm holding my babies, my shoulders aching with fatigue; the next day, God willing, I'm an old woman spinning my cocoon of eternal sleep, oblivious to the life I've created. My husband, with his ruddy cheeks, a beer in hand, becomes a skeleton. My son, racing across the lawn, his elbows pumping, becomes a little skeleton. I think of the unfamiliar future people who will someday occupy this space when all of us are long gone. And who once stood on this grass before we did? What purpose did their lives serve? Who remembers those people now? Then my daughter, who's ten, yanks on my sleeve, sighs, and tells me she's tired and wants to go home.

My favorite death scene in literature occurs when ten-year-old Jane Eyre sneaks into the infirmary to say good-bye to her dear friend Helen Burns, who is dying of consumption. Helen, the only person in Lowood orphanage who has loved Jane and understood her, tries to reassure Jane that the universe contains elements unseen, forces much wiser and stronger than ourselves. Jane responds by asking, "But where are you going to, Helen? Can you see? Do you know?" Helen responds confidently, "I am sure there is a future state; I believe God is good; I can resign my immortal part to him without any misgiving. God is my father. God is my friend: I love him: I believe he loves me."

Jane crawls into bed with Helen and Helen asks, "Are you warm, darling?"

"Yes."

"Good-night, Jane."

"Good-night, Helen."

And then Jane narrates, "She kissed me, and I her; and we both soon slumbered."

When Jane awakens, she finds herself carried off by a nurse. Helen is dead! All of Helen's soothing words have died with her, evaporating in the cold infirmary. Jane wants so much to believe in heaven and God and eternal life, but she cannot.

Once you have a child, heaven begins to seem more appealing. The first night I brought my daughter home from the hospital, I held her in the darkened living room, her eyes flashing moonlight as they shifted furiously from side to side. How alert she was! How much she wanted to see! Soon she'd be using her legs, swaying like a drunk—all those sharp edges, steps, electrical outlets. Don't even get me started on bacteria, parasites, free-floating viruses, and genetic mutations. If, God forbid, she should die, would it be enough to know that her cells will digest themselves and that the earth has a good recycling program through which we will seep back into soil, all of us—humans, marmots, Venus flytraps, cockroaches—connected by some fine universal thread? But how do we tell a child that the "you" in you will simply go dark—*adios, amigo*? Even if the "you" in you lives on inside a clover, a goldfish, what solace is that to the faint of heart?

I don't mind becoming a goldfish, but for my children, I'm

claiming a heaven. So I'm with, you, Helen Burns. I've decided to believe that heaven *exists* and it's the best damned place you ever saw—a place where you're warm and cuddled and loved and you can change into anything you want—a butterfly, a race car. Heaven, I tell my children, is like your best day on earth, but a thousand times better because you know it'll never end, and I'm sticking to my story.

IV

In 1932, at sixteen, Ruth looks like a silent-film star, with wavy black hair, heart-shaped lips, and dark, luminous eyes. She's a skinny little thing, barely five feet tall, but at dances boys flock to her like pigeons. The boys talk her ear off, vying for her attention. She asks questions about their baby sisters, their lame chickens, their uncles missing in action. So they ask to hold her hand, their sweaty fingers revealing their desperation, their immaturity. After the dances, they write Ruth elaborate letters that always begin *My Dearest Ruth*, wherein they profess their head-over-heels love and boast of their willingness to walk thirty miles just to see her again.

Then along comes Ben—a big, strapping fellow who's loud and bold and resembles Clark Gable. He slaps her ass when nobody is looking and pulls her into the cornfields and she does not resist. Maybe because he doesn't ask; he just grabs her and kisses her and picks her up like a real he-man. She feigns disgust, but secretly, subconsciously, this attention is what she craves. Ben pushes her down between the rows of corn and makes love to her, and suddenly she's caught like a fish in a net. Above her she sees a dizzying kaleidoscope of blue sky and cornstalks, the world all in fractals. Here is a man, unlike her cold and remote father, who demands love, commands it, who will announce it brazenly, who will beat on his chest and howl at the moon. How would she have known what she was looking for until she actually found it? How did she know that a girl could get pregnant so easily, and as a result of a few seconds of pleasure would appear a wailing, red-faced baby, kicking in her arms?

After the shotgun wedding, Ben and Ruth move to an immigrant camp in El Monte, California—no running water, wooden-plank floors—but a house nonetheless! Ruth is pregnant again—she's got a baby on her hip, another one crawling on the floor, and the original baby trying to escape out the front gate. Meanwhile, a pot of beans boils over on the stove and some social worker lady is knocking at the door, wanting to talk about "sanitary conditions," and, of course, the baby has just started screaming her head off. Ruth wants to tell that *guera* to get lost, but instead she grabs a rag and swipes at the baby's nose, opens the door, smiles, and says, "Won't you sit down?" and "Can I offer you a cool drink?" She knows how to talk to white people on account of having worked for them for so long, and she will not be perceived as a dirty Mexican or a lazy mother who lets her children run untended like wild dogs.

Where Ben and Ruth are concerned, the real problem is with Ruth's flamboyant younger sister. What man can resist the little sister's self-deprecating charm—the way she laughs at herself and makes lighthearted remarks like, "Oh, silly me!" And how she smacks her forehead so lovably and says, "I am such a dope!" Ruth's sister likes to touch people too; she squeezes their arms and gives a little rub, the kind of touch that gives people goose bumps and makes them yearn to be touched again. Unlike Ruth, the sister douses herself in perfume and sweeps her hair off her temples with Japanese lacquered combs. When the little sister laughs, her cleavage jiggles, while Ruth, so stiff in her demeanor, so prim, so buttoned-up, so matronly, always worries about looking like a floozy.

The houses are so tiny in Hicks Camp, you can't turn around without hitting your elbow against a wall or a window or somebody's nose. Blame the house, blame Ben's lack of will-power, blame the sister, who knows.

Ruth begins hearing rumors and thinly veiled comments from the neighbors, like "Wow, nice of your husband to give that girl a ride everywhere." People start looking at her pity-ingly—the downcast eyes, the gentle, prolonged smiles. For years, Ruth had watched her own mother, Belen, make a fool of herself, losing control in public, screaming obscenities at the other woman, Ruth's father then dragging Ruth's mother home by the hair. Ruth had long ago decided that she would never act so low class; nor would she be made a fool.

Fast-forward sixty years. Ben has been dead for twenty-five years. The younger sister has spent her whole life begging for forgiveness, and each time, Ruth has turned to stone, refusing to acknowledge her. The betrayal of sisters was much worse than a betrayal of husband and wife.

Now at a big family reunion, right in the middle of the mariachis, the buffet, the dancing, the little sister wants to ask for forgiveness again. The sisters are by now very old women, Ruth sitting in her wheelchair, the younger sister wobbly on her feet. The sister tiptoes over to Ruth, tears in her eyes, arms outstretched. People know what's coming, so they make a path, shine an imaginary light on them. Finally—*finally*—Ruth does not look away. This time Ruth nods as if to say, *All right*. Ruth closes her eyes and leans forward—two inches at most—so slightly you have to be standing right there to notice. The sister, gasping, embraces Ruth—a lightning-speed hug—before Ruth can change her mind. Witnesses will later report that Ruth *endured* the hug, and, though she did not actively participate, she did not resist either. The younger sister might as well have been hugging a redwood tree, but, even still, she had sobbed in great cathartic bursts, while Ruth remained stoic. Then some clown probably said something stupid to break the tension, like "Punch, anyone?" Afterward, Ruth would never mention the incident; nor would anybody have dared to ask.

Now we watch as this sister shuffles in to pay her respects to Ruth on her deathbed. It's been a long haul, a lifetime of lost visits. As the "woman who once fooled around with my grandfather" enters, we yawn nervously, stand up, and vacate, leaving the two sisters to their business.

V

We remember this:

Ruth's garden had been a veritable jungle—a jungle dripping with fuchsias, camellias, roses, and rhododendrons—all these flowers thriving under a canopy of ferns and kumquats, oranges and wisteria.

One day, when I was about fourteen years old, my cousins and I had been playing around in the backyard. We were throwing tennis balls to Sancho, my grandparents' energetic little dog, who could catch a mile-high pop fly, every single time, smack in the middle of his jaws.

Somehow the ball had rolled behind the old, rusted-out camper shell, behind which grew an unweeded vegetable garden of withered tomatoes, volunteer corn, and maybe a moldy sunflower or two. We heard Sancho nosing around back there, snorting and digging, so we ran back behind the camper to help him find the ball. Suddenly we found ourselves face to face with a monstrous shrub—a full-grown, thriving marijuana plant (in my mind, elephant sized!), its sturdy leaves and little buds beading up along the thick stalks.

"Whoa . . . is that . . . ??"

"No *way*!" we said, mouths dropping wide open. "What the . . . ?!"

"Oh my God. This is like a dream come true!"

"No *way*!"

"Fuckin' A—it's *huge*!"

We didn't know what to think—that our grandparents led furtive lives, under cover, below the radar. We thought about the meaning of the moment for no more than twenty seconds before we began to organize ourselves—someone to keep watch, someone to act as foil, someone to sneak inside for a plastic bag, someone to clip leaves and buds. I was chosen to harvest—though being naïve, I did not know that I should be clipping the buds, not the leaves. Carefully, I pinched leaf after leaf at its base, gently laying each one in a stack inside a sandwich bag. *Mission Accomplished.* Then one of my cousins got the bright idea that we should sneak into the kitchen and dry the leaves in the microwave, so we could hightail it down to the gully to smoke out.

The microwave was running full blast when Grandpa stomped in and roared, "What the hell do you kids think you're doing?" He snatched the baggie out of the microwave, cursed in Spanish, and shoved it deep into the pocket of his work pants.

Then Grandpa stormed outside, grabbed his ax, and chopped down the whole bush, dragging it mercilessly to the middle of the driveway. He grabbed a can of lighter fluid off the hibachi, doused the entire plant, and then set it ablaze as though it were some beautiful heretic. In the end, all that was left was a sad little black spot on the concrete.

"Don't you dare accuse me of being a drug addict," Grandma Ruth would say. "And for your information, you little criminals, the birds love it." Grandpa refused to talk about it. He'd grunt and stomp off whenever we brought it up.

End of story. *Sigh.* If only we hadn't screwed it up.

VI

Suddenly, then, on her deathbed, as if she's had enough of this nonsense, Grandma gasps loudly, her chest arching, mouth agape. We freeze, terrified, waiting to see if she'll take another breath.

My cousin David surrenders. "Man, I'm getting out of here. I can't take it anymore; this is giving me the creeps," he says.

"Oh come *on*, death is peaceful. It's *beautiful*," my sister Monica scolds.

"How do *you* know?" I snap. "Have you ever died before?" Monica glares at me.

Clearly, after five or six days, we are beginning to get on each other's nerves, and I wonder what Grandma would say about all of us "kids" sitting around her bed like a pack of fools, watching her deteriorate like she was some show on television. The joke is probably on all of us, though. Most likely, she's long gone—sitting on some *From Here to Eternity* beach, sipping from a coconut, soaking up some otherworldly sun—for the first time, unconcerned about the darkness of her skin. Whether Grandpa is there on that beach with her is another subject for debate.

Uncle Benny, her oldest son, has been coaxing her to *go gentle into that good night*. Intermittently he leans over her and whispers singsong phrases into her ear like, "Mama? Daddy's waiting for you up in heaven."

Promises, promises, I think. My own beliefs of happy heaven are quickly dissolving. How does Uncle Benny know? With each passing minute, I want to strangle anyone who presumes to know anything at all about death—all these New Agey know-it-alls. Whatever I'd thought about heaven . . . who the hell really knows?

"Hmph," Auntie Miri grumbles under her breath. "Who's to say she even *wants* to spend eternity with Daddy, after what he did?"

"Maybe she'll meet another guy up there," Cousin Lucy says. "Or another *girl* . . ." someone else says, giving kudos to that possibility. *High five.*

Every little while, poor Auntie Olivia bustles in and leans over Grandma and shouts in her face, "Mama? Mama! Are you hungry?" Olivia stands helplessly, a paper plate filled with food balanced on her hand, blinking and blinking. We know how wrong it is to want to laugh, but Auntie Olivia has that power over us—the bumbling cheerful aunt who spreads misinformation quicker than a wildfire. Watching her blinking like that before her dying mother, for some unexplainable reason, makes me want to laugh my head off. All it takes is one sidelong glance at a sister or a cousin, then suddenly we are in junior high, pressing our hands over our mouths, bowing our heads, peeing our pants, fake crying. It's all becoming so fucking hilarious. The pressure is mounting!

Then we sober up, cough, sigh, and straighten ourselves up in our chairs, suddenly seeing ourselves in Grandma Ruth's place. In Olivia's place.

"When it's my time," one cousin announces boldly, "just do like the Eskimos and put me on a raft and shove me out to sea."

"Eskimos do that?"

"I saw it somewhere. PBS maybe."

"Yeah, when it's my time," another cousin says, "just fucking shoot me and get it over with."

Murmurs all around, and then someone says, "Shut *up*. What if she can hear?"

Then we start bickering about cremation versus burial, which is more natural, which is quicker, which is better for the environment, *blah blah blah*, whether she really wants us all gawking at her, like maybe she just wants to die alone in peace, not like this party in the airport, this striptease of death. We check our watches. Silence.

"Jeez, she's like the Energizer Bunny," Lucy says.

"You ain't kidding," someone else says.

"Takes a licking, keeps on ticking," someone else adds.

"Ha-ha."

And then Grandma Ruth's arm moves. Her foot kicks at the blankets. We gasp. Rush to her side. Her eyes flutter open. "Oh my God!" someone says. "She's coming back to life!"

VII

On the seventh day, Grandma Ruth wakes up.

She's a Time Traveler whose time machine has crashed in the wrong place and the wrong time, and she has not yet learned the language or the customs of the natives. Or, she has been awakened from a thousand-year slumber, like a mummy pillaged from the bottom of the pyramid, the bejeweled mask lifted suddenly from her face.

Everyone crowds around her. "Help me prop her up," my mother says frantically, as they raise her to a sitting position. She stares at everyone, no expression at all.

She's awake! Then we realize: *What the hell?* She hasn't eaten for eight days. Not one crumb of food, not one drop of water. This is a miracle OR a horror movie, I can't tell which.

I start remembering that night when Kristy and I begged Grandma to let us stay up to watch the Monster Rally feature:

Blood of the Vampire (and she did), and how it turned out to be the best movie ever, a movie that begins with the death of the old matriarch, who, it turns out, is really an undead, because after they lay her in the crypt, her eyelids fly open and she smiles, this slow, creepy smile that reveals a set of fangs. The rest of the movie she's sneaking around in this big dark castle, spying on her children, grabbing them and biting their necks until finally someone catches her and chains her up deep in the dungeon, where she wails like a wild animal and claws at her own arms. The central conflict is about deciding who in the family will drive the wooden stake through her heart.

I'm remembering the vampire movie, and everyone is getting all excited thinking that Grandma's come back to life, and the hospice nurse is trying to calm everyone down. He passes out little pamphlets about the stages of death, pointing to one page in particular, a paragraph about something called the final surge. He tells us gently, "This is what we call the final surge—a little burst of energy before they pass."

Some of the relatives gather around her, not caring about the final-surge theory, talking to her like she's just been away on a little trip. They say things like, "Well you sure gave us quite a scare!" and when they offer her sips of water from a straw, she drinks!

Later that night, they carry her to her La-Z-Boy recliner and tuck an afghan around her legs, and I have to say, though I am hesitant to admit this (and call me a schmuck, call me an awful granddaughter), I am getting impatient. Eight days? A thousand good-byes? How much longer can we do this? Even the blue jay has given up.

VIII

When nobody is in the room, I grab a chair and slide up next to her. I can't resist. I lean over and ask, "Grandma, where did you go?"

I suppose I'm hoping that she'll reassure me the way Helen reassured Jane Eyre—that she'll tell me about heaven, about how we'll see each other again. Instead she just stares at me.

Then I try a different approach.

"Hey, Grandma . . . were you dreaming?" I say. Because if she can tell me something, *whoa*, what a dream that would be, right? I hope she will inform me about the interstitial zone where her rocket ship has been hovering. *Speak, oh Time Traveler, speak.*

"Were you *dreaming*?" I repeat.

Then her eyes search my face. She stares at me. She regards me coldly, dispassionate as a lizard. She blinks, not taking her eyes off mine. Then she says just one word. This is the last word she'll ever say to me: "*Ob*viously."

Her voice is deep, disembodied. She stares at me with the distant, regal air of a queen, of a soothsayer, of someone too important to bother with the likes of me.

I ponder the significance of the word *obviously*. What does it mean? "Adverb, Latin. Easily found, seen, understood. Synonyms: evident, manifest, patent, clear." Does it mean nothing more than a simple yes, or does she mean to tell me something deeper, a riddle perhaps? Or did she just mean, "Obviously, I was dreaming, dummy. What else do you think happens when someone is dying, and what sort of question is that anyway?"

IX

On the ninth day, Ruth dies.

She falls asleep and they put her back to bed, and very quickly her breathing sounds like a bird fluttering against her ribs. Finally, as with birthing contractions, her breaths come a minute apart. Shallow gasps of breath. Finally, silence. The end. *Finis. Ex-Grandma.*

We leave the room. Ruth's children gather around her—Uncle

Benny, my mother, Auntie Miri, Auntie Olivia. In glimpses from the hallway, I watch as they hold her, as though she'd just been born, stroking her feet, her hair. They murmur words to her that I'll never know, things I'll never ask about.

Outside the kids are playing, though the sun is setting, and the sky has grown pale orange. My husband, Patrick, has arrived with a plate of *Mexican* chocolate-chip cookies. "I thought your people would need this," he says, referring to "my people" as he always does, perhaps not fully realizing the extent to which he has become my people, that Grandma called him *mi'jo*, my son.

———

Ruth was fourteen and Luisito was three when she found him floating facedown in a muddy pond. She had been washing the clothes when she found him. She hauled him out by the shirt, wiped the mud off his face with her hand, and frantically tried to breathe the life back into him. She pushed on his stomach. She shook him. Nothing worked.

The world turned upside down, spinning on its axis, and when she knew he was dead, it was the first time she thought about committing suicide. She imagined putting a rope around her neck and jumping off a chair. She imagined throwing herself in front of the streetcar. She imagined taking a butcher knife to her wrists. Ruth's father could be sadistic and violent. Ruth's mother, Belen, hell-bent on revenge, kept having babies and turning them over to Ruth, her oldest daughter. Luisito adored Ruth, so much so that he thought she was his mother, and at night when Ruth sang him to sleep, he would stroke his real mother's cheeks (not Belen's) and tell her how much he loved her. He used the word *love*.

Everyone blamed Ruth for the baby's death. She blamed

herself. She should have been watching him. *Stupid, goddamned Good-for-Nothing.* The women washed and anointed the child's body, and later Belen made a big show, wailing and flinging herself across the coffin. Relatives clutched her arms and cried with her.

Dressed in a white suit, Luisito lay on the kitchen table in a small coffin. White carnations and lilies had been placed all around him (good flowers to mask the odor of death). Candles were lit, and prayers were said, and mourners sat in a circle around the table. Ruth's grief felt thick and paralyzing as tar, and she knew that she'd be mired in it forever. Ruth *wanted* to suffer, and she dug her fingernails into her arms as she heard his voice, remembered the sensation of his hands on her face. Then, suddenly, she had this spectacular vision:

Above her brother's body appeared the faces of little children, all of them smiling. Face after face hovered in the air, all of them lingering in an odd light. Then, in the middle of the children, appeared the face of a woman—a beautiful woman with a serene smile and kind eyes. The Virgin Mary? Ruth did not know. She knew only that the woman meant to convey that the boy was safe, that he was in good hands, that he would be happy like the other children. Ruth would later say that this vision had allowed her to live her life, though her brother's death would be the story that she'd most want to tell, the event that would most define her. If she had been a writer, she might have written about it forty-seven different ways.

———

Death arrives as a teenage boy with acne, a boy driving a white newish van with a pink, swirly Rose Hills logo on one door. "Feet first, feet first," everyone cautions him. Some people believe that you want to land feet first in the new world, you want your walking feet, you want good sense, you want to leave this world facing the right direction. The boy lifts her gently onto a white bag and then zips her up. A life lived. A body finished. We watch him push her out on a gurney and slide her in the back of a van. If she had been able, she would have thanked him, patted his hand. We go inside the house and eat our Mexican cookies. Man, it's good to be alive and to be eating cookies. It's good to have a husband who makes cookies, especially when your grandma is dying.

———

Here's how I bury you: think Viking ship, Inuits, a canoe filled with dirt, a black sky, the Milky Way. If there exists a lake big enough, a lake not explored—the other side still being a mystery—I'll lay your body in a canoe at dusk on a bed of rose petals and ferns, your little ceramic frogs placed all around, their stupid smiling faces there to brighten up the underworld. Then I'll forget everything I've learned about everything. I'll light the candles and push your canoe with all my might, believing with all my heart that you'll make it to another shore, another life, where you'll become a butterfly, a race car. I think Luisito is there, and he's very excited to see you.

Riding in the Dark

Typically, I wake up before dawn. I can't help it. Most mornings, my eyes open at 4:45 without an alarm clock, and then my legs start twitching. The best solution I've found to my early morning angst is to get on my bike and start riding. Usually I'll ride my bike in the dark to the base of the mountains near my house, and because the road slants uphill, it's slow and grueling. Each revolution of my feet requires conscious effort, and some mornings I wonder what fool tendencies live inside me to make me want to give up the safety and warmth of my down comforter, all for the thrill of creeping through the darkness like some criminal. I pass through deserted intersections, no need to stop. The only people out now: a few solitary runners, newspaper-delivery drivers, and the random insomniacs. In the silence of morning, the streetlights change from red to green with a low hum and two clicks. Farther up the road, though, it gets wilder. Cars disappear, thank goodness, for nothing spoils good darkness like the shock of headlights in the eyes. The only light comes from the dim amber streetlamps, over which tower cobweb-covered pine trees, over which tower pinpoints of stars. Here I must hone in my senses: my vision narrows to the white disk of light in front of my tire produced by my bike light, and my ears tighten up. If I shift my light upward a bit, my vision expands to a crescent that reveals the undersides of bushes and the full width of the street, but only faintly, as if I'm looking through a thin, lacy veil.

———

Skunks, from what I've seen, don't care a thing about humans. I've ridden close to many foraging skunks, though they barely even glance my way—too busy are they rooting for black widows and earthworms and searching for pizza crusts and rotten bananas in people's yards. Some mornings I'll come upon a skunk—easy to spot in darkness, that white stripe waddling next to the curb, nose to the ground—and I'll ride alongside it until it notices me, evident by a tilt of whiskers and small black eyes in a sidelong glance. If a skunk glances at you, you'd best move away, but slowly, coolly. You've got to love skunks for their adorable natures: one second they're ambling along, cute as stuffed animals, and the next second their tails shoot up, heads draw back and whoosh! A skunk spray is the equivalent of an involuntary scream. And skunks, like absent-minded professors, startle easily. They sink so deeply into their business that they forget to notice the big picture. Then, if one sprays—usually at some rogue raccoon—I'll have to pedal right on through, choking my way into the cloud of doom, no choice but to breathe it in and marvel at the potency of their skunky weapon.

———

Month after month, our sky—tight as a drum with only a few

meager twists of clouds—refuses to rain. Even the oak trees creak and moan with thirst, and if you live near oak trees, you know that nothing short of a blast of napalm can kill an oak. (For years, I've been trying to kill a volunteer oak that's been growing in a bad spot in my backyard. So far, the oak is winning.) The rivers and creeks have dried up long ago. If you knock on the ground it sounds hollow, like an old clay jar.

———

One time, just as I round a bend into the darkest, most strenuous stretch of my ride, three full-grown coyotes appear in my headlight. They stand in the middle of the road, hackles raised, fur billowing in the breeze. What had they been up to? Their eyes glint red as they look at me, a weird, slow-moving mess of helmet and wheels. In previous run-ins with coyotes, they, always skittish, dart off nervously into the darkness—embarrassed almost. But these, these three—they stand their ground. They look perfect as a museum display—poised, regal. How beautiful and how terrifying they are in my circle of light, daring me, almost, to come closer. What dream could be better than this? Anything you see at 5 a.m. has the qualities of the subconscious—both vivid and remote, real and unreal. What if I ditch the bike, grow fur, and run away with them into the canyon? But then there's this: Who would take care of my human children? Who would teach my morning classes if I turned into a coyote and disappeared without a trace?

As I enter pitch darkness, I pull my headphones off. My own ragged breathing fills my ears—that, and the sound my tires make as they grind into the asphalt. I've learned to rely much more on my hearing. My mother, who lives nearby, does not approve of my morning rides, but what can she do? I am an adult, after all. So whenever I'm up here at the scary juncture, I hear her voice: Do you have a death wish? Are you sick in the head? One morning, as I'm struggling along next to a long stretch of foliage—sagebrush, oleander, nightshade—a botanical hodgepodge of native and nonnative, I'm focusing on the illuminated patch of asphalt in front of my tire when I hear a quick rustling of leaves and some snapping twigs. I jump, thinking, What the hell was that? I've never heard such a noise. It's a big noise, and it feels like a warning.

Then I see it. Maybe ten feet beyond my right arm, nestled in some bushes, appears a pair of luminous golden eyes. These eyes, almond shaped and glowering, are big—much bigger than the eyes of any animal I've seen here before. The pale creature crouches low in the bushes, though its eyes remain fixed on me—utterly focused. And it's BIG. Then it registers. In such moments, your synapses fire up, traveling deep and quick into the recesses of your brain like fast-motion root filaments in search of water. In a second, you attempt to connect what you see with what you hear and what you've learned in a human lifetime: tattered library books, *National Geographic*, a zoo cage, a past life, whatever you can conjure up.

Before you: yellow eyes, crouching form. Mountain lion.

Error. Error. Error.

In the time it takes for my brain to spark this thought—five or six seconds at most—I twist my handlebars away in one violent jerk and my left foot hits the ground. I fumble for the pedal as it spins around, and I struggle to regain my balance. Then I hightail it back down the hill, wondering how much pounding one human heart can take before it implodes. Later, I study up on mountain lions and read that they are attracted to moving, sparkling objects, much in the way that house cats lunge at twine and plastic balls. In Southern California, nearly all the mountain lion attacks have been on hikers, joggers, and mountain bikers. Reports of these attacks often include testimony from family members or friends, who commonly note, with surprise, the outstanding health of the victim—how he or she had been in great shape—strong, capable of running. It's the movement that attracts the animal. Imagine the lion's perspective: a clumsy creature ambling up a hill—half-human, half-machine, twinkling lights, squeaking gears—a big fat toy, an invitation to play.

————

Just to clarify: I'm much more afraid of humans than of any other animal. Once I watched a true crime show about a woman out riding her bike in a wooded park when a guy leaps out of the bushes, whacks her with a baseball bat, drags her behind a tree, strangles her, and then steals her bike. What kind of animal does that? One morning a pickup truck, old and rattly, slows, passes me, slows again. Truck stops. Idles. Just me and him and a mountain road. That fucker's gonna kill me, I think indignantly. I know that a very fine line separates stupidity and bravery, but nonetheless, I put my foot down. Literally. My little light shines on his dented bumper. I cross my arms and glare at his rearview mirror. Then I send him my strongest fuck-you vibes. For a minute it's a standoff. Foolish on my part, but I swear I won't move another inch. I'll be goddamned if some sick bastard is going to kill me today, I say to myself. This is for me and for her, that woman who ended up behind the tree. Luckily, the truck rumbles on its way.

————

A popular saying: "It appeared as if out of nowhere." Recently I read about a teenage surfer who was mauled by a great white shark. His friend, who witnessed the attack, told reporters, "Suddenly it [the shark] appeared as if out of nowhere." But really, everywhere is somewhere. Even nowhere is somewhere. Nowhere is the dark space outside the edges of your light, and, most likely, many somethings lie in that somewhere. This is my thinking when it comes to my early-morning bike rides. There is no such thing as out of nowhere. Something can and will appear, and it will have come from somewhere. And as for the poor boy who was mauled by the shark—I see an update in the newspaper that this morning his friends held a funeral at sea. In the sea. In the photo, teenagers sit atop their surfboards at the approximate spot where the boy was torn apart by the shark. They've bowed their heads in prayer, ankles kicking just beneath the waves. But where is the great white shark now? Is he still nowhere? We now know that the great white is, in fact, somewhere. Will a large, shiny, and very visible fin appear, first from a distance, and will it approach slowly, zigzagging though the water? Will those kids on their surfboards then mentally associate a triangular shark's fin with an actual shark? At this point will they perceive danger? Will they then imagine the music from *Jaws*? Will they then swim frantically back to shore? Will they then be safe? If so, we will have a situation in which the shark did not appear out of nowhere.

––––––

In the city, this is how we learn about local wildlife. I spot an unfamiliar bump on the side of the road—most likely an animal hit by a car. As I pedal closer, I see what is, indeed, an animal and that the animal is moving—though unnaturally, as if it is being moved. Quaking. I get off my bike and lean it on its kickstand, positioning my headlight down onto a mass of rumpled, bloodied fur. Dead opossum. Her pointed, opened snout exposes razor-sharp white teeth, and her lips have drawn back in a frozen snarl. But something wiggles beneath the fur on her belly. Her fur shifts and ripples, and for a second I think in a panic: zombie. Then a tiny pink head pokes out from the opossum's pouch. Small as a snail, the pink, hairless possum claws at the air, nudging its head back into her belly, eyes still sealed shut. A few seconds later, another visceral pink head pushes out, and then another. They squirm against her body, mewling, so young that delicate blue veins appear beneath their skin. I crouch low, peering at them. I count seven babies in all. Maybe eight. I can't move. I am looking at the mother's feet—the delicate curve of the nails, the undersides unexpectedly pale and soft. In a few minutes, a car slows and pulls to the side of the road. I hear tires in gravel and a door opens. Footsteps. A man calls out over the running engine, "Hey, is everything okay?"

"Dead possum," I say. "She has babies." The man peers down with me, crouching on his heels, his profile then illuminated in my light. We stare at the squirming, now doomed baby possums. He sucks his breath in. Sighs a slow, soft whistle. "Poor things," he says. "What a shame." As if held there by some force, we keep staring at the wriggling mound of life and death.

"What should we do?" I ask, finally, as if I know him, as if whatever happens will be done together. The man doesn't say anything for a few seconds. He looks apologetic in the spotlight. I think he must be a good man. He shrugs. "Probably best to just leave it alone," he says.

"Yeah," I say. My head agrees: nature will take its course. Still, I wonder how long it will take for the opossum's body to cool, before her warm pouch will turn cold and stiff, and how long those babies will push their snouts at her useless teats, and what it feels like to struggle like that. My heart: pick them up and put them in your jacket pocket. In my dealings with animals, the heart and the head never agree. Finally, I stand up, angling my light back at the road, leaving the dead mother possum and her babies in darkness.

———

You can see the fires burning up the mountains, even from miles away—deep-red, glowing scabs that fester and worm their way lower into the foothills. Riding uphill is difficult now—the smoke is getting bad, and I know I'm stupid for doing it, like smoking three packs of cigarettes in a row, maybe worse. But I can't resist. Coughing and wheezing all the way, I make it to Rubio Canyon. At the top of the closest peak, yellow-orange tongues dart and explode just over the ridge. Bits of burned sagebrush and yuccas drift through the air, the ash falling like snow. Firefighters have blocked off roads and forced residents to evacuate, and when the sun comes up, helicopters will drop loads of red powder over this hill.

———

The bears are coming down from the mountains now. In the paper I read about a guy who chased one out of his garage. I read about a woman who said that while she was cooking dinner, a bear had tried to knock down her front door. The pictures are of overturned garbage cans, claw marks on a tree. My mother tells me that a bear swam in her swimming pool and then took a nap on her patio furniture. She shows me the muddy tracks leading out of the water, the overturned cushions, the bear scat on the grass. On my usual route I find much more bear scat—piles of it that trail back into the canyon. My headlight becomes like a microscope—I pause and note the red berries, bits of fur, gristle. Then, suddenly, I smell something overpowering—a musky, piney, meaty, heavy, barnyard, rotting-grass smell. I hear low shuffling, scuffling, possibly breathing. Here's a phantom, and which part of him I've crossed, I just don't know. He's outside my light now, in the nowhere. How I long for nowhere, but I hop on my bike and get the heck out of there.

————

On my way down, I startle a doe as she stands eating grass in someone's front yard. It occurs to me that those people, these residents of the big city, may never know that a deer visits them in the morning before the first light, not five feet from their front door. The doe trots away in front of me with a funny sideways gait, her front legs and back legs misaligned. She keeps looking back at me, so I wave at her.

Then I coast home at twenty-five miles per hour, wind running through me like chilly river water. In the winter, I'm half-frozen, my chin a veritable ice cube. But this is it, man! I stand up on my pedals, a prayer for the wheelchair bound, and if it's a clear day, sunrise comes—the still-distant sun will paint a pastel streak across the horizon. Then, back on Asbury Drive, I bump into my driveway, dismount my bike, and kiss my handlebars. I give my bike two pats and thank it for not failing me. Call it idolatry, but each morning, that thing saves my life, allows me to widen the boundaries. Later, when I'm standing in front of a classroom, hemmed in, pacing before the chalkboard, I will recall the darkness and the edges of everything.

In Defense of the Rat

M y daughter wanted a hamster—or some creature to cra-
dle in her hands, one that would nuzzle its whiskers
against her nose, take a peanut from her fingers, and perform
somersaults across a little trapeze. We already had two dogs
and a cat, and we didn't need another pet. But then, who really
needs pets? Isn't it the other way around? I'd always envisioned my children growing up in a household filled with creatures great and small—motherless squirrels, broken-winged
blackbirds, or trembling little mutts rescued from lethal injec-
tion. I envisioned my future home as a delightful cacophony of
barking, meowing, chirping. In my mind, the boundary
between the animal world and the human world is blurry
indeed. I pity children who've never owned a single pet—the
ones who stiffen in a dog's presence, hands plastered at their
sides. I feel sorry for kids conceived in the cold digital age,
more comfortable holding a joystick than a kitten. My children,
I vowed, would stroke the velvet noses of horses, and they
would laugh with delight (not cry) when a dog slopped a pink
tongue across their faces. And how vast is the animal world!
Consider the beauty of the elephant as she sways under a hot

sun, her nimble trunk grasping at a carrot. Consider the sheer freakishness of a praying mantis as it performs tai chi and spreads its wings before eating its prey.

However, I knew that hamsters were not an option.

When I was ten years old I had a hamster named Oscar. At first Oscar seemed as adorable as a miniature Teddy bear. He burrowed beneath his wood shavings, then popped out and ran a few laps on his little metal wheel. He kept me company while I sat at my desk doing homework, and I was soothed by his scratching and nibbling and the *click-click* sound as he pried open his sunflower husks. Sometimes I'd push the tip of my pencil through the bars of his cage and let him nibble on the wood.

Oscar seemed lonely, though. Sometimes he just sat in a pile of wood shavings, staring at nothing in particular. How can we truly know ourselves if we cannot look into the face of our own kind?

My mother somewhat absent-mindedly agreed to a second hamster (though she vowed never to touch the damned things and promised that if she ever saw one running around loose in the house she'd vacuum it up). So, without a second thought, I bought a wife for Oscar and named her Olivia. I imagined that Oscar and Olivia would fall in love and raise a little family together, just like the characters in a Beatrix Potter story. When I first pushed Olivia into Oscar's cage, they sniffed each other curiously like a couple of old pals.

Then I ran off to play and forgot about them. The next morning, I found Olivia (or what was left of her) lying motionless in the middle of the cage. Creeping closer, I saw that all four legs and her entire head had been gnawed off down to the vertebrae. All that remained of Olivia was a bloody, beheaded stump.

Oscar, that little cannibal, sat in one corner staring coldly at me, intermittently licking his paws and rubbing them across his blood-streaked cheeks. It was like a horror movie wherein a supposedly well-adjusted family member suddenly goes berserk. But perhaps I was to blame for pushing the two hamsters together too quickly. After all, how would I like it if a mysterious hand from the sky had suddenly shoved a strange person into my house? Or maybe, I reasoned, the cage had just been too small and Oscar had simply been guided by instinct to protect his territory.

Not long after that, when my family went on vacation, my aunt agreed to take care of Oscar. My mother drove me to her house, and I brought along the cage and a bag of supplies— aspen shavings, food pellets, and wood chews. A week later, when we returned, my aunt showed me the empty cage. "He escaped!" she said. "When I tried to pick him up, he bit my finger and then ran after me and started attacking my feet! I didn't know what else to do. . . . I panicked, so I grabbed the broom and swept him out the back door. He's a demon!"

And that was the end of Oscar, as far as I know. My daughter would not be getting a hamster for her birthday.

"Maybe we should try a rat," I said to my husband, Patrick, who just happens to be a medieval historian. "That's funny," he said. "You're hilarious."

Try mentioning the word *rat* to a medievalist without conjuring up visions of Europe besieged by *Rattus rattus*, circa 1348, the beginning of the Bubonic plague.

"I know, I know, it sounds crazy," I said, "but I've read that rats make excellent pets. They're very intelligent and you can train them to do tricks and . . ."

He only narrowed his eyes at me and refused to discuss it further.

———

I decided to begin an official campaign for *Rattus rattus*. Every day, in an attempt to erase those images of the Black Death, I e-mailed Patrick pictures of cute rats I'd found on the Internet: a rat wearing a little bowtie and tuxedo; a rat wearing little pajamas and holding a little Teddy bear; a rat wearing a bonnet and pushing a miniature baby stroller. He would respond by sending me a picture of a house cat holding a dead rat in its jaws. (We had a cat.) I retaliated by sending him a heartwarming YouTube video about a cat and rat who became best friends, even sleeping side by side. I sent him the true story of a rat that saved a coal miner's life—squeaking frantically and leading the man to safety moments before the mine collapsed. I pointed out that actually, it was the fleas living on the rats that had spread the plague. (Rats were victims too!) He sent me movie trailers for *Willard* and *Ben*, in which rats take over the world.

Finally Medieval Man relented, though not happily. "I'm not cleaning the cage," he said, "and I refuse to touch them."

"No problem!" I said cheerfully. "You won't have to do a thing!"

———

At the pet store, after Mira had chosen the rats—two spunky young black-and-white females—the clerk asked, "Pets or food?"

"Pardon?" I wasn't sure if I'd heard her correctly.

"If they're pets," she said, "I'll put 'em in one of these little boxes. But if they're food, I'll just throw 'em in a paper bag." She gave me a little wink.

"Oh," I said. "Yeah. These are pets."

She nodded. "Come on girls," she said sweetly to the rats, "you're getting adopted!" She placed them in a cardboard pet carrier imprinted with the smiling faces of rodents, then folded the lid shut and handed the box to Mira, who looked as though she'd just won the lottery.

Back home, we set our new pets loose in their trilevel "apartment," complete with hammock, wheel, and plastic igloo. After living in a drab aquarium, these animals could scarcely contain their joy. Scrambling from the floor to the top of the cage, they'd leap again to the bottom, like circus performers. Zipper and Calico bonded almost immediately with Mira, and when she held them, they climbed onto her shoulder and peered out from behind her mass of frizzy hair. I found this maneuver both cute and mildly alarming.

Mira and her four-year-old brother, Leo, couldn't have been happier. Together they built obstacle courses and mazes and trained the rats to climb ropes and to use a simple pulley they'd created with yarn and cardboard. (Even Medieval Man seemed impressed, though he still couldn't admit defeat.)

———

Of course, my children did not know the history of rats. Unlike mice, who are typically portrayed as lovable and funny, like Beatrix Potter's Mrs. Tittlemouse or Kate DiCamillo's Desperaux, rats aren't often the protagonists of children's literature. When they appear, they are seldom lovable and rarely exhibit any positive characteristics. Even in *Charlotte's Web*, in which E. B. White favorably portrays a pig and a spider—two creatures with a history of bad press—the rat, Templeton, is cunning, dishonest, and stealthy. For as long as humans have been around, we've been trying to keep rats out of our houses and away from our children. What could be more alarming than a wild brown rat sneaking into a baby's nursery or sniffing around in the kitchen cupboards?

Now here were my children, picking up the rodents and then letting them crawl on their laps, their shoulders, their necks. Despite the historical evidence, the rats were quite docile, even . . . dare I say . . . affectionate? Never once did they bite a finger. They learned to respond to their names, tilting their heads in response to our voices; they made eye contact. In fact, they behaved very much like little dogs.

———

One day, almost a year later, we noticed that Calico had begun to walk with a strange, sideways gait. She constantly tilted her head. She stumbled in her cage. Once, she almost fell off Mira's dresser. I didn't say anything to Mira, but I knew these symptoms couldn't be good. Calico's eyes had begun to bulge.

A few days later we found Calico huddled in the corner of the cage. Her feet were clenched and she would not eat or drink.

"We've got to take her to the vet!" Mira insisted.

"She might get better," I said hopefully.

"Mom!" Mira wailed. "How can you just let her die?"

"You're mean!" Leo said, crossing his arms.

Of course I did not want our rat to die. I did not want her to suffer. But I'd already Googled Calico's symptoms and I believed that she most likely had a brain tumor. I'd read that pituitary gland tumors were very common in domestic rats. I'd even perused autopsy photos from veterinary websites, and I could practically see the pea-sized tumor right through Calico's small skull. Her bulging eyes would tell almost any veterinarian what I already knew. Plus—most importantly—it was the end of summer. Without my teaching paychecks, we were facing lean times; we simply could not afford to spend $100—at minimum—for a trip to the vet.

Some might argue that allowing a creature to suffer is inhumane. But I had recently sat with my grandmother as she died. For nine days, my mother, aunts, and cousins stayed close as her body diminished and her consciousness dimmed. I realized then that death is a mysterious process, much like birth, and that there is value in helping someone during that process, seeing them through to the end. We could see our rat through it too, I thought, help make her comfortable. I didn't want my children to be afraid of death, or for them to think of it as something that happened behind closed doors. Besides, something surprising had begun to happen. Zipper, the healthy rat, was tending to her dying companion, like a nurse. Zipper brought Calico peanuts and bits of food, then pushed shredded newspaper and wood shavings around her ailing sister to keep her warm. It seemed wrong to take Calico away from her companion.

As I expected, Calico deteriorated rapidly. During that last week, she would lift her head and look at us with sad, defeated eyes. When she saw us, she whimpered softly, as though she knew that something was happening to her body, something she couldn't understand. She seemed sad to be leaving us.

By the last day, the rat's eyes were sunken and her breath was shallow and quick. When Mira walked into the room, Calico lifted her head and started to make a rhythmic chirping sound, like weeping. She seemed to be asking the human she'd known and trusted to hold her. She seemed to be saying good-bye.

"You can pick her up," I said. I tried to project motherly calm, but inside I was panicking. I didn't know if I'd be able to find the right words to comfort my daughter.

"Are you sure?" Mira asked.

Tears rolling down her cheeks, she lifted Calico and cradled her gently in her palms. Within minutes, the rat had what appeared to be a seizure; when it was over, she seemed calmer, soothed by Mira's touch. We sat together for the next two hours, watching the rat as it lay dying. Mira asked tough questions about whether I believe in God, whether animals go to heaven, whether people go to heaven, and why people hate rats so deeply.

Again, the rat's body tensed, stiffened, and then relaxed.

As I watched my daughter weeping over the rat, I thought about these small pariahs and the dangers they face: exterminators, poisoned pellets, snapping traps, laboratory experiments. And now, one of these stealthy survivors had bonded with a human who had grown to love it. How can we help what we are? I wondered. Did the rat ask to be born a rat?

Finally, after one violent spasm, Calico stopped breathing.

Her whiskers stopped twitching. Her four chewing teeth—now exposed—looked sharper and more yellow than I'd realized. Her limp claws looked like small hands, pink and downy, with creases across the palms like a human.

I found an empty Kleenex box and laid the rat inside. Leo ran out to pick some geraniums. Perhaps I was too quick about wanting to dig the hole, but I was exhausted. We were all exhausted. Had I been a better mother, my children would have written little messages on scrolled-up paper. I would have suggested that they each say a prayer before we lowered the rat slowly into her grave. Had I been a better mother, we would have taken a handful of dirt and thrown it upon the box. *Ashes to ashes, dust to dust, Saint Peter protect this creature.*

But we'd all been on edge for days. Our vigil had worn me

out, so I simply opened the box and placed the rat named Calico inside the hole. Now that she was gone, I felt a great sense
of relief. "Good-bye, Calico!" I said. "Say good-bye, everyone!
Does anyone want to say a prayer?"

Leo, quite the handyman with a shovel, quickly filled in the
hole. Happily, he stomped the dirt, jumping up and down as
Mira became hysterical.

"Mom!" she wailed. "How *could* you? What kind of funeral
was *that*?"

"Ashes to ashes, dust to dust," I said gently. "It's more natural this way, right?"

"She's cold in there! She needs to be wrapped in something.
. . . Let me dig her up . . . she needs a proper burial!" Mira
grabbed the shovel from Leo and started to redig the hole.

"Heeyyy!" Leo yelled, shrieking in protest. "My hole!"

"Oh my God, can you stop her?" I begged Patrick.

"But she's cold," Mira sobbed.

"She's dead, honey," Patrick said. "Her spirit doesn't need a
body anymore."

The American Academy of Child and Adolescent Psychiatry
recommends that children be allowed to bury a pet, to make a
memorial, or have a ceremony. Mourning takes time, the psy-
chiatrists say, advising parents not to immediately replace the
dead pet.

But a few days after our little funeral, when Mira was still
sobbing and I didn't think I could take it any longer, I did a bad
thing. "Listen," I said. "How about we go to the pet store and
buy a new rat?"

"Really?" she said softly, between sniffles.

"Yay! A new rat!" Leo yelled. "I want a white one! I want a
white one!"

Patrick shot me a look. "Are you crazy?" he mouthed. I shrugged. Maybe I was crazy to want another rat. But I couldn't stand to see Mira falling apart. I reasoned that a new rat would console her, and had anyone even considered the feelings of the surviving rat? Rats, like humans, are social animals. Zipper would need a new companion!

When I remember my own childhood and envision the one I want for my children, more than ever, I imagine a veritable "March of the Animals." How much easier life would be without all these creatures who require food and water and walks around the block (we've walked thousands of miles), not to mention old age and illness—the arthritic paws, the failing kidneys, the special diets, and, finally, having to say good-bye. But I would have it no other way. Someday when my children are grown, I'll see our animals marching by, a whole parade of them: rabbits, ducks, hamsters, a hermit crab, cats, an assortment of dogs, two mice, a school of goldfish, and, finally, the rats—pariahs no more!—twitching their whiskers and grinding their long yellow teeth with happiness.

Bloodyfeathers, RIP

Ten minutes into my remedial writing class (Sentences to Paragraphs), and students were already falling asleep. I'd been hired to teach at Merced College, a town right in the middle of California's agricultural belt, and I'd been teaching for less than a year. I stood at the front of the room scrawling sentences across the whiteboard while the air conditioner, cranked up to full capacity, emitted a mind-numbing hum that had caused everyone to go slack-jawed. One hundred eight degrees was not unusual in Merced, and it was the kind of weather that made you want to kill somebody. Anyone looked at you wrong and you found yourself lunging for the throat—especially if you were some poor bastard who lived without an air conditioner.

Then the classroom door creaked open, and against the white-hot valley sun appeared the silhouette of a Sasquatch, wearing an army jacket in spite of the 108-degree heat. His long, frizzy hair—shaved violently up one side—made him look like he'd been blasted out of some postapocalyptic war movie. A series of tattoos snaked up his neck—tattoos with blurry edges of no particular pattern, most likely the product of a hot needle and a ballpoint pen.

Twenty-eight heads turned to see what had arrived. The wild man wore big boots but carried no books, no backpack—but with him came a cloud of crazily vibrating molecules that created a strange, unsettled energy. As he lumbered to the front of the room, a sudden gravitational compression occurred, or the air pressure changed somehow, as students flattened themselves into their desks.

"Sorry I'm late," he said, dangling a pink add slip between his big, callused fingers. He leaned in close, smelling like days and days of cigarettes, and then whispered, loud enough for everyone to hear, "I should probably tell you that I just got outta prison. My parole officer said this would be good for me."

Here we go, I thought, but I nodded, pointing to an empty seat and rambling on about transitions or some boring thing, though I'm sure nobody heard a word I said, myself included. Our newcomer took his sweet time getting to his seat. Before he sat down, he paused and looked around the classroom with a slow, steady grin that revealed smallish nubs of teeth that had either stopped growing when he was six years old or had been filed down on purpose. Somehow his face, too, seemed small and disproportionate to the rest of his body, like some man-boy hybrid, a ten-year-old locked inside a man's body.

When he was good and ready, he kicked the chair away from the desk, scraping it against the linoleum and banging around as he arranged himself behind the desk. He made a big show of checking out his petrified classmates—male and female—one by one. Then he took a long look at each student, raising his chin at them, saying, "Hey" to those who would look back at him. The other students, all of them smaller and younger, mostly averted their eyes, and for once, miracle of miracles, kept their attention focused on the sentences in their books.

At the end of class, I glanced at the add slip and was surprised. "Bloodyfeathers? Is this your real name?"

"That's what it says on my birth certificate," he said, barely moving his mouth, unblinking. Thick round glasses blurred his eyeballs, so I couldn't tell if he was staring at me or beyond me.

"It's Native American," he said in monotone. "My dad wanted me to have a warrior's name so I could beat the shit out of people." A little ripple went through the classroom, and students were staring at me and waiting for the inevitable train wreck. Of course I didn't know what he'd do.

"What, you never heard a Native American name before?" he said, looking all around and glaring at the class.

"Hey, man," I said, "we're all brothers and sisters here." Sometimes I said corny things like that, and I actually believed them. And with that, he seemed to relax.

I hoped he would tell me that he went by a nickname like Bobby or Louie or even the initials B. F. or even just Feathers, so that I didn't have to say the word *bloody*. Then I imagined the practical application of the name: "Bloodyfeathers, what is the difference between an adjective and an adverb?" "Bloodyfeathers, what is the topic sentence of this paragraph?" "Bloodyfeathers, is this the correct use of an apostrophe?" *Bloody* was not an association I wanted to make with a recently released prisoner, especially an ex-convict who was sitting in my classroom with what I then realized was a swastika tattooed on his neck.

The term *remedial* has been replaced with words containing less emotional baggage—names without implied failure and without any hint of the words *dumb* or *slow*. Just like that expression that dog lovers enjoy repeating—"No bad dogs, only bad owners!"—many teachers today will claim that there are no dumb kids, only incompetent teachers. Now those classes are called Basic Skills or Developmental English or Emerging Skills, but really those words all describe the lowest classes available, many that teach skills that students were supposed to have learned in elementary school.

In Merced, Basic Skills English: Sentences to Paragraphs consisted mostly of Hmong and Latino students—most of them eighteen years old, many of them embarrassed by their accents and hunched over their desks, and also a few goofballs or "troublemakers" who may in fact have had legitimate cases of attention deficit disorder or undiagnosed learning disabilities. Though most had graduated from high school, the average student in this class wrote at a fourth- or fifth-grade level, at best. Many could barely read. In these lowest classes, students are often people whom other teachers have given up on.

Soon, however, I dreaded going to that class. We met four days a week for an hour and fifteen minutes each period, for sixteen weeks total. In teaching terms, that practically made us a family. That's a lot of hours. I tried to focus on students like Maximus Xiong or Gustavo Arellano or Mai Vang—sweet kids who were just trying to make up for lost time.

In class, Bloodyfeathers hadn't done anything wrong—not like he'd held some kid up by the ankles and shaken him down for pocket change, and not like he'd held us all hostage or pressed a box cutter into some kid's neck—nothing like that. With him, though, had arrived a cloud of darkness—a heaviness—something that I believe we could all feel, a sort of magnetic force field. You felt it when you got near him, like the resistance between two negative poles.

He tended to overreact to the slightest sound—a door slamming, someone coughing. When someone volunteered a comment, Bloodyfeathers would twist around in his seat to leer at the person who dared to speak, his eyes ablaze. At all times, he was ready to give his classmates a high five or to inform them of their idiocy, depending on whether their comments fell in line with Bloodyfeathers's dog-eat-dog ideology. He reminded me of a wolf boy who'd wandered out of the forest after years of living with canines and was now trying to mimic human behavior.

"Hey, fuck you guys," he said one day to the entire class, slamming his fist down on the desk. "You people don't know jack shit about jack shit."

"Whoa, what's this?" I'd said. He was sweaty and acting twitchy. He wore weight-lifting gloves and kept cracking his knuckles.

I pointed to the door. "Take a walk, please."

"I'm fine," he said.

"I need you to take a walk," I said, again. I shot him laser beams with my eyes, mentally pushing him out of the room with a block wall that I'd created in my head. He sighed loudly, rolled his eyes, and stood up, toppling his chair. On the way out I heard him mumble to one of the students, "Punk ass."

I can't remember what had set him off, but it was something fairly minor. In English 81, students loved to voice their opinions—often quite boisterously—and they enjoyed any discussion that was not about grammar. Bloodyfeathers, however, had a short fuse—or maybe no fuse—but I figured as long as he didn't harass or threaten other students, and as long as he deferred to my authority, I was willing to accommodate him. Otherwise, where's an ex-con to go? How would he ever find a job and create a life on the outside? Plus, I really, truly believed in the democratic philosophy behind the community-college system. Welcoming immigrants with their blank notebooks and dull pencils, as well as welfare mothers with four children, the community college seemed so distinctly American—to represent what was best about us. If Emma Lazarus once imagined Liberty to have said, "Give me your tired, your poor, / Your huddled masses yearning to breathe free, / The wretched refuse of your teeming shore," I had similar beliefs about an open college system, the "lamp beside the golden door" representing enlightenment that would lift students up and help them live better lives.

But I had not imagined Bloodyfeathers. He seemed oblivious to my daily torment and seemed to be enjoying his new schoolboy persona. Clueless about how to act in a classroom, he turned to the other students for cues. When they opened their books, he opened his book. When they took out pencils, he patted down his coat pockets and then asked to borrow one. He completed his homework and never missed class. Other students kept their eyes tightly focused on their books, nodding at him politely if need be, but for the first few weeks, it felt like an interloper had moved in, like a squatter had taken possession of our classroom, and we weren't quite sure how to think of him any other way.

Though I was relatively new to teaching, I'd already learned a few tricks for diffusing volatile people in the classroom. One is to react with perpetual kindness—to be so sweet that nobody would dare to cross you. Another is to try to see everyone as they might have looked when they were babies wearing their diapers and pointing at birdies up in the trees, before they'd been humiliated and turned upside down and the world had made them vicious. The rationale: if you can see someone's inner child, then you can see their true nature, not the social constructs—you can start fresh. But that trick doesn't always work. Maybe Adolf Hitler was never a baby, if you know what I mean.

Teachers must never allow students to become zombies—those

glazed eyes, that half-dead stare. One day I noticed that I had a roomful of them. My usual routine was killing them. It was killing me. So much emphasis on the parts of speech and basic grammar rather than the process of writing and the freedom of expression had taken its toll. Where was the joy? What about communication? What was the point of all this? I felt their pain.

"Let's write a story," I said.

"About what," they said suspiciously.

"Whatever you like," I said, doing a little tap dance.

I needed to see their pens flying across the paper, so I asked them to write about a memory or something beautiful or something terrible, and I wanted them to describe it as accurately as possible and with as much detail as possible. "No grammar rules," I said. "Just be free and write without stopping!"

As the saying goes, be careful what you wish for.

After they'd been writing for a while, Bloodyfeathers raised his hand and said, "I would like to read my story to the class." Now the students were awake.

I thought about it for about five seconds, trying to quickly anticipate what could go wrong. "Okay," I said weakly. Then I got nervous, realizing I had no idea what words would come out of this guy's mouth or what demons lived inside his head.

Reluctantly, I moved aside as he shuffled to the front of the room and then squinted at his own words, as if someone else had written them. He cleared his throat and peered at his paper. He had written a story in the third person, describing himself from afar as a child of hard-core Hells Angels. He painted a chaotic picture of a boy's childhood—bikers snorting cocaine on the coffee table, guys beating the shit out of each other for fun, pit bulls roaming free, strangers sleeping on the couch, and the boy—that weird little man—everybody's punching bag.

As with most remedial students, his writing skills did not

match the depth of emotions he wished to convey, so he began to ad lib, adding details about the kid's love/hate for his parents, about all the crazy drug-induced shenanigans, about how the boy had been led to trouble and eventually to prison—all this he said looking at his paper only sometimes, and finally ignoring his paper altogether.

Students sat spellbound as he described life in prison and coming to this class after serving a twelve-year sentence—his entire adult life. He'd enrolled in college to get the probation officer off his back, but then again, he just might stick it to that moron and anyone who had never believed in him and get himself some kind of degree. Paybacks to those who had ever called him a dumb, worthless piece of shit, and maybe now he would prove those assholes wrong, and anyway, he didn't want no minimum-wage job, didn't want to work for the man.

"Damn," someone said. "What'd you do, dude?"

Nobody moved.

Bloodyfeathers turned to me.

"May I?" he asked with the exaggerated decorum of a Victorian gentleman.

"I suppose," I said.

He took his time. He did a little head roll. Bent his fingers back one at a time. Sighed.

"Killed a guy," he said, finally, sniffing the air and peering at his fingernails, his glasses glinting with sunlight. "Stabbed him in the neck." He waited for a reaction.

Of course I knew this confession had no place in English 81. I knew I shouldn't let an ex-convict be the guest speaker in my English class (at least not until I'd gotten to know him better). But this was a rare diversion and certainly not the norm. Here was an element of storytelling that seemed to have a connection with writing and self-expression. This was real life! Plus, maybe having Bloodyfeathers in class was like a *Scared Straight* program for the rest of my students.

If he could keep Gustavo or Maximus out of prison, then maybe here was a lesson more valuable than anything I could teach about paragraph development and subject-verb agreement.

"I had no choice!" he finally blurted out. "I had to do it! Crazy dude was coming at me with a knife and it was me or him." Then he talked for a few more minutes about that night at the bar, the trial, the sentencing, about being eighteen years old and getting thrown into maximum-security prison, what a nightmare.

"Prison sucks," he said in the end, as he gestured wildly. "All I learned was how to be a better criminal. And that is the moral of my story."

The class applauded and someone said, "Good job, man." He jerked his body around left and right, pleased with himself and enjoying being the center of attention, his frizzy hair shaking with the conviction of a rock star. Perhaps it was my imagination, but it felt like some of the heaviness—that black cloud—had lifted. Still, I couldn't know for sure if he was telling the truth, but even if he wasn't, it was a good narrative. And if he was telling the truth, his behavior made more sense to me—this anomaly of a man, forged from chaos and schooled by fellow criminals. I remembered, too, that my job was not to judge but to teach—to give this man a small door that he could walk through.

So when most students wrote two-page vignettes about a grandma's funeral or getting a new puppy or winning a soccer game, Bloodyfeathers wrote twelve-page, single-spaced survival accounts of his childhood. His accounts were sometimes rambling and digressive, but I wouldn't have stopped him—I couldn't have stopped him—just the way you can't stop a snake from shedding its old skin.

About ten weeks into the semester, Bloodyfeathers stopped coming to class. His seat sat empty day after day, and I'd be lying if I said I was disappointed. Students drop courses all the time because of jobs, family obligations, loss of interest, change of heart. The semester ended. No longer did I dread coming to class, and my step felt lighter. The students wrote their exams, dropped their blue books on my desk, and disappeared forever. Then the class was over.

"So long, suckers," I said to the chairs.

End of story.

Not end of story. One night at around 2 a.m., the phone rang. I still had one foot in a dream when I answered it. A woman's voice said, "Collect call for A. Morales from Folsom State Prison. Will you accept?" I blinked hard, trying to clear the cobwebs from my brain and remember if I knew anyone in prison, like some cousin or a distant uncle. Did I? No, I did not.

"Will you accept?" the voice said again.

"No!" I said and quickly hung up.

"Who would be calling you from prison?" Patrick wanted to know.

"No clue," I said.

The next night, the phone rang again at 2 a.m., and the same woman's voice said, "Will you accept a collect call from Folsom State Prison?" I was annoyed, not so much that some prisoner was calling me but that this person had the nerve to call me collect. Did this person think I was a millionaire?

"It's that prisoner again," I whispered to Patrick, with one hand over the receiver.

"Give me the phone," he said. "Let's get rid of this asshole."

"I'll do it," I said. Then I said, "Yes, I'll accept the call."

Static and then a voice.

"Hey, Teach," the male voice said blandly, like it was just another day. The walls seemed to be creeping inward. I felt like I was floating in a dark landscape, looking down at our little house as it twinkled in the night.

"Who is this?" I said.

"It's Bloodyfeathers. Remember me? Bloodyfeathers? How's it goin', professor?"

"Jesus, Bloodyfeathers," I said. "Why are you calling me in the middle of the night? Why are you calling me at home? How did you even get my number?"

Then Patrick's eyes were bugging out and he was trying to wrestle the phone from my hands. Patrick had heard plenty of stories about the infamous Bloodyfeathers. "Give it to me," he kept saying, "Let me talk to him."

"No," I whispered fiercely. "I can handle this."

"I just had a question," the voice said sadly. "I gotta know why you failed me. Why'd you give me an F?"

"What? Why did I fail you?" I said, clutching the phone and blinking hard. "You failed yourself. You stopped coming to class."

He sighed long and hard. "I know, I know. I'm a fucking idiot," he said. "I screwed up again. Got picked up on a parole violation."

"How did you even get my number?"

Bloodyfeathers sighed. "I wish I could see you," he said. "But I really called because I needed to tell you that YOU are a really great teacher. You are. You changed my life. Believe it or not, you are the first person who really listened to me. You did. You treated me like a human being."

"All right," I said, "thank you."

"Shit! Were you sleeping? I'm sorry!"

Patrick had turned on the light and was sitting up staring at me. I pointed to the phone, shook my head.

"I'm hanging up now," I said. "Don't call this number again, okay?"

"Can I at least write you a letter sometime?"

"Uh . . . sure. Send it to the college."

"Okay. I hope you have a nice life."

"You too," I said. "Good-bye, Bloodyfeathers."

"Jesus Christ!" Patrick said after I'd hung up the phone.

"I know," I said.

Patrick, I could tell, had wanted me to command Bloody-feathers to fuck off. He had wanted to me to say something like, "Stay the hell away and never contact me again." To say, "How dare you invade my privacy? I'll call the police if you call me again, so don't you even think about it!"

And logically, that is what I should have said.

But I had come to think of Bloodyfeathers as a person, not a monster, and I'd seen glimpses in his rough writing of that little boy who'd been tossed around.

And the thing about teaching is that sometimes the boundaries get blurred. Hundreds of people sit before you, the best of them open to your words, to your ideas. If you do your job right, with any care at all, whether or not your students can write a sentence matters. Whether or not they can communicate matters. In they come, their minds awash in a haze of ideas that do not appear clearly as distinct black-and-white sculptures in the white room of the mind—they cannot see the slither of the *S* in the word *serendipitous*, for example, or the order of letters like soldiers lined up in tight formation. The sentence matters. Each individual word matters. The right words in the right order sparkle. There is a beauty in the sentence that you see and they don't see, and your job is to make them see. Sometimes, when the sentences line up and the words become three-dimensional, they seem true, an emotion resonates, and a story begins to emerge from the mud, and you can stand in front of that class, even those slack-jawed students, and dance around them until they wake up. Literally, you dance around, and you clasp your hands and you write waves and curlicues and slanted lines that mean something all across the board. And who cares if they get As (they won't) or even Ds; what matters is that they see (even blind students can see) that the English language is a gorgeous mixture of history and irregular conjugations available for old, young, black, brown, broken, whole, sad, ecstatic.

So if Bloodyfeathers, by way of the telephone line, had crept into my bedroom, I believe that he was simply yearning for another glimpse of what he might have seen inside the classroom. His longing had nothing to do with me, personally, but rather something more to do with the recognition that ideas are bigger than we are and that all those ideas floating around above the chaos and the chatter contain both volatility and purpose. Writing must have helped him make sense of how he fit in. As Joan Didion wrote, "I write entirely to find out what I'm thinking, what I'm looking at, what I see and what it means." And in the words of Montaigne, "I have never seen a greater monster or miracle in the world than myself."

If there exists an English teacher who enjoys grading papers, I've never met her. Most teachers will tell you that all the magic happens in front of the class and that the rest is paper work and drudgery. Recently, sitting at my desk and imprisoned by stacks of papers, I suddenly thought of Bloodyfeathers. I wondered what had become of him.

Here is a new verb: to *Google*.

I Googled him, knowing that he couldn't be too hard to track down with such a name. Within seconds, an obituary appeared. The words were maddeningly vague—no care for the form, the meaning of the words themselves. Maybe the people from the mortuary had written it up—just the facts, all business, no love.

Bloodyfeathers, it turns out, had died a few years after the phone call from various health problems, though, of course, the obituary did not specify exact causes. With a little more digging around on the Internet I found a picture he'd posted of himself looking much scarier than I'd remembered. In the years since I'd last seen him, he'd become a Juggalo, which essentially means that he was a grown man dressed like an evil clown, that he lived the lifestyle devoted to the band Insane Clown Posse. Apparently a whole subculture revolves around the Juggalo mind-set, which, according to Wikipedia, includes drinking and spraying the inexpensive soft drink Faygo; wearing face paint, generally like a clown; making and responding to "whoop, whoop" calls; and expressing a (generally) tongue-in-cheek obsession with murder.

Had he lived, I believe his evil-clown phase would have passed. I can understand its appeal, though, for it provided him with a new family, fellow Juggalos and Juggalettes, or in Spanish, Juggalas.

I pondered his life for a moment and wondered if I'd taught him anything worth knowing, and then I wondered if he'd taught me anything worth knowing. And if so, what?

Maybe writing connects us to people with whom we'd otherwise have no connection. The writing may not make us kindred spirits; nor does it improve our character or erase crimes—but it connects us, and thus we develop empathy. When my students give me something they've written—that is, a piece they seem to care about—I try to hear the voice behind the words, and I try to accept what is being offered to me. When the story is very personal, they're almost asking, "Do you see me? Did this really happen?" In the act of reading, you are saying, "Yes, I see you, I have heard you, and I know you exist."

On Bloodyfeathers's Myspace page—words that have outlived him by years—I find a note written by a friend, a guy with whom he'd started a band called Anarkiztik. The friend posted his message after Bloodyfeathers's death, which seems as good an outlet as any for grieving, a direct line to heaven. (And how do we know that such messages floating around in cyberspace do not reach the deceased?) The language of the note is rough and distant. Not English exactly, but some hybrid, filled with yearning to belong to something, somewhere. Still, it's got heart and energy, and it runs ragged with grief.

Translation:

Damn, Ninja, shit isn't the same with your ass gone. It's like my vocabulary is gone. I can't write or even fucking think of any rhymes and it pisses me off too. Fuck you for dying on me! No, I'm sorry, Ninja; I just miss my homie. I know you're up there chilling by a lake of Faygo and I am glad that you are out of pain and can see now. I miss you, Ninja. Just please send me something to write about. I'm just numb. I really miss you, Ninja. Help your Ninja out a little bit. I'm going to fuck this world up when Anarkiztik goes worldwide, Motherfucker. I love you, homie, and may you rest in peace

A theory: This Buddhist once said that when you meet someone, it's taken lifetimes to get to that moment. He said that each person who crosses our path is significant in some way, though we may not understand why until a later lifetime. Sometimes people walk into your life; they walk out again. Do we assign too much significance to these lives that randomly crisscross ours, or not enough? I'm sure I've done both. In those criss-crosses, though, it's the few words, the sentences that I give them and they give me—little gifts that burn up and float away—that will connect us and buoy us along like little rafts right through this lifetime and into the next.

I'd be lying if I said that I hope to meet Bloodyfeathers in the next lifetime. Most likely, I will. But for today, here's to Bloody-feathers, eternally chillin' by that lake of Faygo, that lake of orange soda, an electric sky overhead, and the power of the wild world all around him.

The Girls in My Town

I

Here in the Central Valley—in this sun-bleached, hardtack landscape—we have no choice but to search for beauty. The soil, dun-colored and rock-hard, erodes into a soft layer of silt that covers the town every time the wind blows. All across California's farm belt—this land between the Sierras and the Pacific—rows and rows of cotton bolls, apricot and walnut trees, grapevines and tomato plants, roll out for hundreds of miles. But then the rain ceases. Two years pass. Three years. Early morning dew brings the smell of manure, which lingers in our neighborhoods, a smell that grows stronger with every passing month. Winter brings no rain but only a thick layer of tule fog, which traps us further in a damp, white haze. Bitter particles of pesticides hang in the air. We drive on Highway 99 in search of something to look at and find For Lease signs, abandoned Western-themed restaurants, and peeling billboards advertising brand-new housing developments that never panned out—a picture of a two-story tract home adorned with a Spanish-tile fountain, a father holding a plump toddler, a chemical-green lawn, a happy yellow dog. Between aqueducts and waterways, mazes of irrigation canals and ditches, we try to improve our minds. We enroll in classes at the community college and vow, once and for all, to see it through.

But our library—a big, sad building—houses old, second-rate books, and the librarians seem tired as they thumb through ladies' magazines and gaze wearily over the tops of their reading glasses. This library, unlike some libraries—with summer reading programs and cheery children's wings containing beanbags and puzzles—is not a happy place. Here, the hours are limited. Erratic. Now think of the brutally hot sun. You worry about dogs not having any shade. That dog chained to some little leafless tree in the back of somebody's junkyard. That dog whose water bowl is covered in green slime and sits about six inches from the end of his leash. You worry about dogs and children. (Cats can generally take care of themselves.)

II

Francisco, a beautiful boy, sits at the front of the classroom—center stage. When the girls arrive, they circle around him and slip into desks nearest to him, glancing his way and trying not to giggle every time he makes a comment. He leans forward with folded hands, his feet planted solidly on the floor like some goody-goody schoolboy. When he asks a question—usually something ridiculous—the girls turn completely around in their seats to stare at him. I say, "The midterm exam will be next Tuesday at ten—don't be late!" And he raises his hand and asks stupidly, "Uh . . . Miss? Is there a midterm for this class?" Then one of the serious, not-so-beautiful boys murmurs, "*Pendejo!* Open up your ears," and beautiful Francisco will wink at me and yawn. His eyes, translucent and emerald green, make me uneasy. He resembles Johnny Depp but speaks with a slow rising cadence that reminds me of my grandfather—my grandfather who ended up with seven kids and a gambling habit. Francisco tries to flirt with me by calling me *profesora* in that lazy melodic lilt, though around here—at age thirty-two—I am old enough to be his mother. I wonder which girl will get to him first and then whether he'll pay child support or if he'll want to get married *ever*, being so beautiful and all.

III

Our neighbors across the street, whom we call the Meth Joads, remind us of Steinbeck's Joads because they drive around in a patched-together pickup truck that teeters under the weight of a perpetual mass of junk: wooden pallets, broken bicycles, miscellaneous car parts. Unlike Steinbeck's Joads, however, they are most definitely meth addicts, with the telltale tense jaw, the broken shorn-down teeth, the deep bronchial laugh that inevitably turns into a coughing fit. The Meth Joads have a teenage daughter who sits on the front porch and talks on the cordless phone. One day she's out there talking and I notice that Misty Joad's belly has grown big as a watermelon and is now straining against the seams of her tank top. A few days later, Mr. Meth Joad hauls in a yard-sale crib from his pickup truck. "It's all good," he says, straining under the weight of the crib, a cigarette between his teeth. The girl, Misty Joad—no more than sixteen and heavily pregnant— paces the sidewalk and talks languidly on that phone like she's waiting for somebody to pick her up and take her some- where. Every few days a red-faced teenage boy shows up and the two of them drive away in his Mustang. Then the boy stops coming. Eventually Misty Joad walks the sidewalk with her newborn baby. But imagine her power. Even with dirty bare feet and no plans, her body has declared a coup: *If you won't love me, here's a person who will.*

IV

We live down the street from the continuation high school. When we first moved to the neighborhood, Patrick and I referred to it as the Bad-Boy School because that is what my grandpa used to call the school on his street in Boyle Heights. At that Bad-Boy School in Boyle Heights, enormous pigs lived belly-deep in black muck—muck that emitted an odor so foul that we tied bandannas over our noses and gagged anyway as we rode our bikes past the pigs' enclosures. I'd spy on those bad boys in their rubber boots as they shoveled muck and slops, and I was glad that, being a girl, I would never have to shovel shit or get my ass bit the way that Grandma had once been bitten on the ass by a rogue hog (after it had chased her around the neighborhood for a good forty-five minutes). That pig had gone *hog wild*.

The Bad-Boy School in this town, though, turns out to be a Bad-*Girl* School, with a special program for pregnant teens. Sometimes I see those girls exercising on the track—twenty or thirty of them—a whole herd of teenage girls walking around in circles, hands supporting their lower backs, bellies sticking out a mile. Merced gets hotter than hell, so usually the girls pant dramatically and fan themselves, periodically squinting and shielding their eyes from the merciless sky. After their babies are born, most of these girls will come back to school for a few months, and then the majority of them will drop out of school altogether.

I push my own baby in her stroller and observe the girls through the chain-link fence as they complete their one-mile forced march. One starts brushing her hair. The teacher cajoles her, and momentarily she quickens her pace, but as soon as the teacher turns around she slows down again. Looking at them, I try to imagine the moment of love or rage or revenge that brought them here. Most of their babies' fathers will not marry them. Most will continue living in poverty as single mothers. The majority of their children will have learning and behavioral problems. Some of those babies will end up right here, back on this very same track.

In the Teen Parent Program, girls are taught life skills, like how to eat healthy foods such as carrot sticks and cottage cheese rather than a *machaca* burrito (two out of three girls are Latinas) and a three-pack of Hostess Ho Hos. (And who knew that a bacon guacamole Whopper had 1,020 milligrams of sodium and 43 grams of fat?) They watch filmstrips in which fetuses unfurl their tiny limbs; black guppy eyes grow human eyelids; a prehistoric fin separates into ten toes. Later the girls learn about scary conditions like preeclampsia and gestational diabetes, and suddenly they understand why so-and-so's cousin gave birth to that extraordinary thirteen-pound infant, the one with doughy, waterlogged skin and a protruding tongue.

They learn how to change a diaper and how to hold a baby's head so it won't bob off to one side. They learn about the soft, downy triangle called the fontanel and how their babies' brains, soft as cream cheese, can be felt by gently placing a finger on that eerie soft spot. They learn about shaken baby syndrome and sudden infant death syndrome, and then they are given stickers with emergency contact numbers—school counselors, social workers, paramedics. They are told that they will not be alone and that caring for a child requires both strength and humility. *We are your support system*, the girls are told. *We are here for you.*

Across the street from the Bad-Girl School, on the corner of Twentieth and G Streets, Rollins' Donuts emits the thick, cloying scent of golden doughnuts as they bob around in the fryer.

After school the girls disregard what they've learned in health class and line up out the door, shifting their pregnant selves from foot to foot while absent-mindedly massaging the undersides of their bellies, bellies now covered by maternity jeans with spandex tummy panels. Some girls, the rebels, forgo the secondhand maternity clothes altogether (too *old ladyish*!) and let their bellies hang over the elastic bands of their sweat pants.

Just downwind from Rollins, at the government-approved WIC grocery stores, girls can cash their WIC vouchers for Similac, double-wide boxes of Cheerios, and big hunks of cheese.

In the hospital after my daughter was born, the nurse had brought me yet another stack of forms to fill out. "Here," she'd said, handing me a pen. "You'll definitely want to fill these out." I hoisted the baby onto one shoulder, and just as I had begun to write my name in the first box, I saw that I was about to fill out a Women, Infants, and Children assistance application.

"Oh, I don't need this," I said. I tried to give back the pen, but she wouldn't take it. "Oh but you *have* to," she said. "You get free food like bread and milk and formula. Formula's expensive! You'll see! You can get WIC vouchers until the baby is five years old! Imagine five whole years of free food!"

"No, that's okay, really . . ." I said again. She pressed on.

"Why the heck *not*?" she said, leaning close, giving me a conspiratorial look. "Almost everyone gets approved. Well, just think about it."

After she left, I crumpled the forms and shoved them into the trash can. Certainly, I thought, WIC is for *very* poor women—single mothers, teenagers, and migrant farmworkers. Being of sound mind and body (or so I tell myself) and having a job, I knew I would not need such assistance, and now I admit to being slightly offended that the nurse had automatically assumed that I needed WIC at all. Based on what? Based on my dark hair and my last name? But in her defense, the odds that a Latina with a newborn baby would need government assistance are, in this town, indeed very high. Here, population sixty thousand, one in four women and children are enrolled in WIC. That's a lot of formula. A lot of cheese.

Every day, on my street, little girls push strollers with real babies in them. The girls walk with their friends—other young girls with *their* babies—sometimes three or four of them at a time. They walk shoulder to shoulder in the middle of the street like they belong to a fertility parade. Sometimes, we have to drive around them, swerving gently to the opposite side of the road. "Careful," I'll tell Patrick, as he turns the corner. "It's a stroller brigade." It's an evangelist's nightmare. (Or would that be a dream come true?)

Times have changed since my grandmother and great-grandmother (with sixteen children between them) dodged the shame of being dark and young and pregnant. Without reliable birth control, access to good schools (only the inferior "Indian schools"), or decent jobs with decent wages, what choices did my grandmothers have? Even if girls did not have babies of their own, they often became mothers by default—by tending to younger siblings, nieces, and nephews. Babies were a fact of life. The wealthy had nannies and nursemaids at their disposal. My grandmothers *were* these nannies.

Fast-forward a hundred years and observe the very same girls—now unfettered by husbands and tradition—now walking side by side in the middle of the street, chattering away as they adjust their babies' juice bottles, talk on their cell phones, and halfheartedly dangle little rattles above the strollers. Unlike my grandmothers, the girls in my town have access to birth control pills, integrated schools with specialized programs, and guidance counselors who are supposed to tout the merits of college—even to the brown and black kids. The girls in my town have more choices, though some people might argue that when you're young and poor and your own mother lives on welfare, those choices are hard to find. Love, on the other hand, is easier to find. Love (or the promise of it) is free. Love makes you feel good, even if only for a few minutes, especially if you've never had a father. Love is beautiful: think of walking hand in hand with the green-eyed Francisco at sunset along some fictional beach. And if you end up getting pregnant, *We are here to support you.* And here's a fact about babies: babies now come with many cute accessories—headband bows for little bald heads; Lilliputian T-shirts imprinted with hip slogans like "Ladies Man" or "Change My Diaper, Biaatch!"; knit caps with built-in Mohawks and bunny ears; pacifiers with vampire fangs painted on the mouthpiece.

V

The obstetrics nurse at Mercy Hospital dims the lights and draws the threadbare curtain across the center of the room, a flimsy illusion of privacy between me and my fourteen-year-old roommate. Both our babies had been born around midnight, and now, with babies swaddled and sleeping inside plastic, wheeled bassinets, sleep seems like a superb idea.

Everyone has gone home, and I'm alone for the first time with my newborn daughter. I can't stop staring at her. She'd been the loudest, angriest baby in the nursery, apparently furious at having been exiled from the womb. With our bodies now separate entities, the world, to me, seems upside down. Sharp edged. Somewhere, a car smashes into a tree. Airborne bacteria and spiky pollens float past. And who is this little human, anyway? What about her life comes predestined? I try to see the tiny, scrolled-up map inside her skull—the grid within her brain, the catalog of her choices, and, ultimately, her destiny and desires: an aversion to crowds, a deep compassion for animals, a love of money, a penchant for mathematics, a blind left eye.

Meanwhile, my roommate and her boyfriend are lying side by side in bed and watching back-to-back episodes of *Cops*. Crack addicts make excuses, a homeless woman sobs over a lost dog, a teenage girl's baby daddy just put a steak knife to her throat. My roommate's baby daddy adds his own running commentary: "*Damn*, look at that dude! He's so fucked up. *Hey! Remember when the cops beat the shit out of my uncle?*" My roommate murmurs something in reply. And what's going through her head? I try to remember being fourteen. I try to imagine being a mother at age fourteen.

Then my roommate's baby starts crying. The crying gets louder. Pretty soon the baby wails like a peacock. Ay-*ya*! Ay-*ya*! Suddenly, the sound of a crying baby makes me feel crazed, like an animal with its paw caught in a trap about to gnaw off its own foot. My head throbs. My spine aches. I wonder if these fourteen-year-old children know what do with an infant. Do *I* know what to do with an infant? How will we keep these babies alive? How will these children survive the years ahead? *Jesus, where the hell are the nurses?* I think. I consider saying something, but I'm too exhausted. I've got seventeen years on her, and compared to her, I'm already an old lady.

VI

The Lamaze teacher said, "Visualize that your uterus is a beautiful spring bud, slowly unfurling its leaves, blossoming right before your eyes." This teacher talked so gently about the body and the birth process—how childbirth happens every single day, how women's bodies are designed for birth. Her voice, like a drug, hypnotized me as I sat cross-legged with the other pregnant women—some with husbands, some with boy-friends, some with their moms. We breathed deeply and traced slow circles across our bellies—a technique that supposedly calms the body, calms the mind.

At the onset of my labor, then, I successfully envisioned a Georgia O'Keeffe orchid, a soft swirl of violet petals and leaves. As labor progressed and the pain intensified—surprise, sur-prise—my orchid melted away and in its place appeared an engulfing blackness. Eventually, as the pain intensified into lightning bolts, a creature took shape—half-man, half-goat, with horns, red eyes, and lobster claws, the whole bit; he could have leapt right out of a Francisco de Goya painting. By the eighth hour, the beast had burst right through the floor and had me around the waist and was trying to pull me into the hole that had opened up in the middle of the floor.

Lying in my hospital bed in the small-town Catholic hospi-tal, I decided to surrender myself to the image; in other words, I would not swim against the current and try to turn the demon back into an orchid. Instead, I would face my nightmare head on: I would grab that son of a bitch by the horns and peer directly into his flaming eyes. *Ha! Two can play at this game*, I thought. Here's what the Lamaze teachers don't tell you about childbirth—particularly childbirth without drugs: the goal is not really to stay calm and focused; the goal is to stay *alive*! Once, when I was eighteen, a fortune-teller peered at my palm and said, "Mmm . . . lucky you live in *these* times. One hundred years ago you would have died giving birth." In this small-town hospital, though, one hundred years does not seem like that long ago.

So with the fortune-teller's words echoing in my head, I told myself to fight like a warrior. Screaming felt good. I screamed until my throat became sandpaper. Suddenly, a nurse grabbed me by the wrist and said sternly, "Dear. You are wasting an awful lot of energy on all that screaming. Why don't you get ahold of yourself? Just *calm* down." I jerked my arm away and glared at her. How dare she tell me how to have a baby? How dare she intrude into my hallucination? Anyway, I thought, she had no idea what she was talking about—all those Lamaze lies, all that childbirth propaganda designed to shut us up, to keep the masses *sedated* so that nurses and doctors don't get headaches.

So I decided that with each contraction I would scream every bad word I knew. *Bitch, motherfucker!* I didn't care what anyone said, not Patrick, not my mother, not even the nuns. It felt good to fight then, to unleash my rebellious tongue.

Later I wondered about my fourteen-year-old roommate, who had been giving birth at the same time. Why had I not heard her voice? Did she not feel such intense pain? Had she been given an epidural? Was *I* too melodramatic—me with my death-defying warrior fantasy? Now I wished I'd talked to her during those two days that we'd shared a room. We talked a little bit, but she averted her eyes. Painfully shy. Not much of a talker. I wish I'd asked her how she got through it and whether she dreamed up some flower or some other beautiful thing. What thoughts and images travel through the mind of a fourteen-year-old girl as she becomes a mother?

VII

Carl Jung believed that his schizophrenic patients' hallucinations should be treated with the same respect that one might treat any "real" scenario that one can see with one's own eyes. Jung believed that if a person truly believes that he is being chased by wild tigers in a jungle, you should not remind him that he is actually sitting in a comfortable velour armchair and not running for his life through a jungle. Nor should you tell him that the tigers are simply phantoms or figments of his imagination. Instead, you should help him *to survive*. Instead, ask him, "Have you a spear? Have you a rifle?" Urge him to jump into the river or to grab a big stick. In acknowledging the phantom tigers, Jung believed that he could reaffirm and validate the contents of a mind, those contents being significant in their symbolism and necessary to the survival of their host.

VIII

Here is a true story that has become part of our local mythology:

Late one night, sixteen-year-old Benita Ramos pounds on the door of a random house. Crying and begging for help, she says that a man has just kidnapped her son—snatched the stroller right out of her hands. When police arrive, Benita explains that she had been visiting the baby's father (age seventeen) at his parents' house, and as she was walking home and pushing the baby's stroller down the dark path, a tall, skinny white guy tackled her from behind and then ran off with the stroller, her baby boy still strapped inside.

That night, Benita appears on the eleven o'clock news, slurring her words and begging for the safe return of her baby. Her family—aunts, uncles, parents—all stand behind her with grim expressions on their faces. The girl's story sounds plausible because terrible things happen to children in our town. Imagine a place of planetary misalignment, a celestial crisscross of weird energy. Imagine the Bermuda Triangle on dry land. Our town, home to the Pitchfork Killer and the Yosemite Killer, makes us believe that anything is possible.

Later that night, though, police find the empty, overturned stroller on the muddy embankment of the creek. In the flashlight's white beam, they spot what looks like the baby's body floating facedown in the black, stagnant water. (Bear Creek, a tributary of the Merced River, begins high in Yosemite back-country; up there, it's gorgeous and rugged and the water rushes across car-sized boulders, all framed by Douglas firs, sugar pines, and sequoias. Look up and see an impossibly blue sky with fast-moving wisps of vaporous clouds.) But here, far away from the creek's source, the baby's hooded sweat shirt is caught on some protruding branches next to an overturned shopping cart. (God only knows what else is down there.)

Eventually Benita confesses, though detectives observe that she is not very articulate; moreover, they say, she acts much younger than a girl of sixteen. Later, by piecing together her confession and forensic evidence, they'll determine that Benita tried to drown the baby in the water fountain at Applegate Park. They'll say that she then threw her baby into the creek and faked the kidnapping.

After this happened, we will always think of Benita's dead baby when we go to Applegate Park, which functions as our town center; we go there most Sundays. Fragrant orange and pink rosebushes surround that fountain, and nearby, children can visit a half-blind donkey at the petting zoo or an old bear that paces his enclosure for eighteen hours a day. If Benita's baby boy had lived, surely she would have brought him to ride the miniature train that circles the perimeter of the same park in which she killed him.

But Benita won't say more. She appears to be a broken girl. Detectives claim that because she appears to be mentally disturbed and because she functions below the level of an average sixteen-year-old, they might never get inside her head. What's there to say when you have a baby at age fifteen and your seventeen-year-old boyfriend starts dating some other girl, some little slut from another high school, and now your

160

whole life consists of Pampers and plastic baby bottles, milk-encrusted rubber nipples, and maybe once in a while your life gets supplemented by a *Jerry Springer* episode and an orange Popsicle?

"I just went sort of crazy," she might have said. And, "Having a baby is like, really, really, hard. Nobody understands." And if you can love babies when there's nobody else to love, sometimes you hurt babies when there's nobody else to hurt—you don't mean to exactly—you just can't control it. Maybe it's payback for all that's ever been done to you.

IX

Our mothers tell us the story of La Llorona, which means the Wailing Woman. In the story, La Llorona's husband leaves her for another woman. After being rejected and abandoned, La Llorona plots her revenge.

La Llorona decides to take her children on a picnic next to the river. She brings a quilt and a basket filled with strawberries, hard-boiled eggs, heart-shaped cakes, and honey water (because she really loves them). Imagine a spring day resplendent in all ways: the children play in the tall grass, they laugh, they tumble around.

But, oh, what bad luck to have been born a child of La Llorona! (How many times, for how many hundreds of years, have these children had to endure the same fate with variations in details?) Soon she lures the children, one by one, through a low tunnel of shrubs to the river—probably across a raccoon or deer trail. The tunnel, enshrouded by eight-foot-tall reeds, leads to a waterside thicket; here frogs lounge on lily pads and dragonflies dive-bomb the water's surface.

Then she drowns her children, one by one, and afterward, she arranges their bodies side by side across the family quilt and kisses each of them in the middle of their cold foreheads. Later, when La Llorona's husband finds the children, his screams can be heard for miles. She's dragged away in chains and put into a dungeon, where she wakes up in shock and realizes what she's done.

For all of eternity, she will cry out for her dead children. After she dies, her ghost will wander the riverbanks in search of new souls. Our mothers tell us that if we look carefully, we can see La Llorona crouching next to the water, furiously rubbing her hands with sand and gravel. They say that if we listen at night, we can hear her moaning and rattling chains. If we're not careful, they say, she might mistake us for her dead children.

Our mothers never talk about any moral of the story. They tell it because it's a good story and they can alter the details as they please. But children are presented with the idea of mothers gone crazy, of mothers who use their children to get revenge. Many children have nightmares about La Llorona because all our basic fears can be traced to our mothers, whether we realize it or not. During the day, she combs our hair and kisses us. At night, she's the madwoman in the attic. It's this duplicity that scares the hell out of us. All mothers have dual natures, and La Llorona's pale face and leaf-strewn hair remind us of this. So we dream about children floating beneath gentle currents, their faces obscured by the water, their small, icy hands floating to the surface. The simple lesson: Stay away from water! Don't go out after dark! Be quiet and go to sleep! The deeper message: Do *our* mothers want to kill *us*? Is it not a question of *if* but a question of *when*? And most importantly: If our fathers abandon our mothers for the Other Woman, should we opt out of the picnic next to the river? (We get these thoughts especially when walking next to creeks or canals or irrigation ditches.)

X

Once a girl brought her infant to the final exam. She arrived late, all sweaty and exasperated, and I don't remember exactly *why* she brought the baby—probably because her mother couldn't babysit, so I said, "Fine, fine, sit down, take the exam, don't want you to fail on account of that," knowing these girls have enough problems as it is. So I offered to hold the baby throughout the exam; I jostled it about as I walked up and down the aisles patrolling for cheaters. It was weird because suddenly I became a mother, teacher, grandmother all at once. I lost a little bit of my authority. I became a relative. A regular person.

Midway through the exam, when the baby started to fuss, I poked the baby's mother on the arm and whispered, "Do you have a bottle?" She dug around in her backpack and (thank goodness) found one. I gave the bottle to the baby while students were bent over their exams. The baby sucked down its formula, making that gulping sound that babies make. They study you, their fat little fingers fondling the edges of the bottle, fondling your fingers, reaching for your nose, their bare toes. This one never took his eyes off me. Once he snapped the rubber nipple with his four teeth and then laughed loudly. The class heard this and then laughed too. The baby wanted us to love him, maybe to improve his chances of survival.

How quickly the border between classroom and home, personal and professional can dissolve! But it felt good to hold a baby in a classroom. I could breathe for a minute. A baby provides comic relief. A baby is funny and random and unscripted. But I could not fully enjoy the moment, because the whole time I was wrestling with ideas like, Is this really a good message to be sending to students? Shouldn't I send her away, saying, "No children allowed," because those are the rules? Will this baby distract the other students? How much do you bend the rules for these girls with their babies, these girls with the odds stacked so high against them?

XI

My teenage students have babies right in the middle of a semester. The San Joaquin Valley has the highest teen pregnancy rate of any region in the United States. My students call me up and say, "Miss, I just wanted to remind you that my baby is due in a couple days . . . so if you don't see me in class . . . that's why." Then they disappear for a couple days and then reappear, their eyes slightly glazed. "Back already?" I say, because after my baby was born I'd staggered around for two weeks feeling like I'd just completed the Bataan Death March. But for most teenagers the body heals itself and springs back into shape almost immediately; life goes on. Evolutionarily speaking, a quick recovery makes sense. Biologically, humans can give birth at a relatively young age; consider that, on average, girls begin to menstruate at age twelve—sometimes as young as age eight. But to what advantage? Do species evolve to produce as many offspring as possible, even at the risk of mothers being socially and mentally immature? Is it better to throw our DNA into the mix as often as possible to improve the odds that at least some of our genetic material will survive? Consider, though, life within a tribe—all those hands, the elders to keep watch, to give advice, to admonish. Perhaps for some humans, the young-mother model works just fine. But without the tribe, without rules, who will watch over the girls in my town—these girls who often need mothering themselves—these girls with their babies in their low-rent apartments with boyfriends who sometimes marry them, most often do not?

After class one girl says proudly, "Look, miss. I can already button my old jeans!" She holds up her blouse to reveal her small, swollen belly. Any evidence of her pregnancy has all but disappeared. Who would know that an eight-pound baby had recently been expelled from that same body?

At times, I'm baffled by the lack of impact motherhood seems to have upon many of my students. Many girls don't appear to be visibly moved by the event of childbirth. Or at least they don't know how to express their feelings about it. After they return to class, I search, but I cannot discern any real change in their eyes. "So? Well?" I say. "How did it go?" The girls often shrug. "He weighed nine pounds," they might say, or, "He's already sleeping through the night, miss." They'll tell me details that they've heard other mothers say, common quips that you hear on TV or in doctor's waiting rooms—bland, unrevealing details that seem scripted. Many of these same girls want to write essays about the births of their babies, but they almost always lack the language to express anything more than a basic plot outline. Example:

> My water bag broke right in the middle of the grocery store. It felt so weird. My mom drove me to the hospital. They put me in bed and got me all hooked up to the machines and then the pain got really bad. It went on for hours. They ended up doing a C-section, thank God. The labor lasted over twenty hours but then the baby was born healthy and now I am so happy. I love my baby so much!

In the margins of their papers, I'll press for specific details and analysis: "Describe the pain! Describe the baby! Do you feel any different? What obstacles do you face now?"

XII

My cousin X and I practically grew up together. Sometimes she'd stay at our house for seven, eight, nine days, and then I'd stop talking to her. I'd give her the cold shoulder. I just wouldn't talk anymore. She'd say, "Are you mad at me?" I'd shrug. "Are you sick of me?" she'd say. "A little," I'd say. I didn't know how to articulate that I needed my bedroom back. I needed to close the door and read and think. I was that kind of kid. I needed solitude to feel normal. Sometimes I would just lock my door and stay in there the whole day. I'd stare at the ceiling. I remember saying, "I just need to think," not really knowing what I needed to think about. Then she'd say, "Okay, I'd better go home then. I guess I'll call my mom." I loved X the way only cousins can love other cousins, kids who are thrown together in this world by way of shared mothers, mothers who some-times turn parenting into an informal commune, the philoso-phy being: you take them today, I'll take them tomorrow. The mission statement being: together we will keep these children alive. X's mother had gotten pregnant when she was eighteen years old. The guy ended up marrying her, and then a couple years later he dumped two-year-old X and my aunt onto Grandma's front lawn. He tossed their clothes out of the car and all over the grass. Then he drove away. End of story.

So we understood why X got pregnant at age eighteen. She started looking for love in all the wrong places—love with surfer guys with names like Travis and Dave. One day she got herself kicked out of her house and she moved in with us. "I just can't have an abortion again," she told me. "I won't do it." The born-again Christians had gotten ahold of her, pressing antiabortion pamphlets into her hands, pamphlets that con-tained gruesome pictures of dead fetuses, their tiny hands awash in fresh blood. She'd convinced herself that her other baby was waiting for her in heaven and that, for the time being, the baby was being cared for by angels, who had it gently by the hand, and that one day it would be reunited with its Mommy-on-Earth, but only if Mommy-on-Earth was willing to call herself a sinner and change her wanton ways. "I'm having this baby," she said defiantly. It was a common trope back then.

But babies get annoying real fast. They get bigger and then they squirm away from you and then they call you names like *butthead* and they take off their shoes and hurl them at you, and as soon as you get the shoes laced up again, they pry them off and toss them behind the dresser, and inevitably you lose that shoe, and now you've got four mismatched shoes without mates. Toddlers can be hard to take, especially when they start saying NO all the time and that's the only word they know. They poke you in the eyes when you're sleeping and you're dead tired and they always have runny noses and the snot runs into their mouths and they lick at it with the edges of their tongues or smear it onto damp encrusted sleeves. They jump on you when you don't expect it, knees and elbows jamming into your ribs, into your chest, into your cheekbones, and the more you try to wrench them off, the more they want to jump on you again; sometimes you want to shove them off and maybe pinch their little arms or yank a clump of hair or leave them in the crib, even if they're crying and calling you so pitifully, and you know this borders on child abuse, but it's really hard when there's no father and you are *it*—the kid's sun and moon.

XIII

My daughter and my fourteen-year-old roommate's daughter—both born on the same night, the same hour—are thirteen years old now. When I look at my own daughter, I cannot believe that a girl of roughly her age and temperament could be a mother. She slams doors. She stomps around. She throws up her hands and says, "Are you *kidding* me?" She sketches pictures of horses and then crumples them up. She announces, "I'll take animals over people *any* day" (and she means it). And although her fingers are now longer than mine—her hands, more graceful—I cannot, no matter how hard I try, imagine those hands changing a diaper.

Do our daughters have anything in common? My roommate's daughter, according to county statistics (based on her mother's age and ethnicity), will very likely have a baby before she turns eighteen. Then the girl will most likely drop out of school and struggle to care for her child in this place of leached soil turned to clay. My roommate's daughter may never know about the migratory waterfowl, such as Canada geese and whistling swans, that once stopped off in our valley marshlands—most of which have been drained to rechannel water for irrigation. And maybe the babies, in some weird way, reflect our need to find beauty, once again, in this landscape. In any case, I suspect our connection to the land runs deeper than we know.

As for our daughters, the fortune-teller might peer into her crystal ball or examine our girls' palms and see a whole web of alternate realities. "Anything can happen," she might say. For all of us, the road is wide open.

Acknowledgments

I am grateful to the editors of the following magazines in which these essays first appeared:

1966: A Journal of Creative Nonfiction, "The Big Divorce"
Arts & Letters, "Nine Days of Ruth"
Baltimore Review, "Gunslinging"
Chattahoochee Review, "Bloodyfeathers, RIP"
Harvard Review, "One Small Step"
Hobart, "The Burrito: A Brief History"
Literary Mama, "In Defense of the Rat"
Los Angeles Review, "An Elegy (and Apology) to Dogs I've
    Loved"
River Teeth, "Riding in the Dark"
Southern Review, "Chief Little Feather, *Where Are You?*"
Southwest Review, "The Girls in My Town"
Under the Sun, "Skin and Toes, Ears and Hair"

"The Girls in My Town" also appeared in the *California Prose Directory* and *Best American Essays 2013*.

I am deeply indebted to Joe Mackall and Dan Lehman of *River Teeth* for supporting this manuscript with the River Teeth Literary Nonfiction Prize. I am also indebted to Cheryl Strayed, who helped this manuscript see the light of day and who is an inspiration to women writers everywhere. Also, I am ever so grateful to the University of New Mexico Press for adopting my "odd children" and giving them a home.

I am grateful, also, to Professor Emeritus Carl Klaus, founder of the University of Iowa's Nonfiction Writing Program, not only for his mentorship and support but also for his scholarly and inspirational works of nonfiction, which have guided my writing from the beginning.

Furthermore, I am grateful to all my friends and family for their support, especially Esther Morales, Linda Morales, Monica Morales, Delmira Miovsky, Jennifer Niren, Kristy Raney, and Gabriella Gutierrez. Thank you, Dana Christy, for being a tireless reader and true ally.

But most of all, thank you to Mira and Leo Conyers, my little earthlings, for expanding my heart and giving me daily insight and empathy. And to my sweet Patrick, my anchor, for all those glasses of celebratory champagne, for making a big deal out of this, and for giving me all the love, time, and space to do my thing.

—AM